D0870661

1—Mallards

THE MALLARDS
AND THEIR NEIGHBORS

Old Homestead Tales Series

The

MALLARDS

and Their Neighbors

by NEIL WAYNE NORTHEY

Drawings by William Wilke

ORGINALLY PUBLISHED BY:
PACIFIC PRESS PUBLISHING
BOISE, ID
RE-PUBLISHED BY:
A.B. PUBLISHING
ITHACA, MI
COVER ART AND DESIGN BY:
JAMES CONVERSE
COPYRIGHT 1998

Contents

Introduction

THIS is another story of the Old Homestead, and especially about the little Wild Creatures that lived at the Duck Pond on the Old Homestead. You have met a few of them in the story about *The Bluebirds and Their Neighbors,* but most of them are new acquaintances.

You see, the Bluebirds and their neighbors were mostly Furry Friends and Feathered Friends, who lived near the Grand Old House, or in the Apple Orchard, or along the Hedgerow, or at the Rambling Old Barn, or in the Little Jungle Thicket, where Molly and Peter lived. But the Mallards and their neighbors lived at the Duck Pond, and along Little River, which flowed through the Old Homestead. They liked to play in the water and among the Fuzzy Cattails along the Marshy Banks.

Perhaps you will think that some of the Mallard's neighbors were not kind to them and that is true. Many times even Fearful the Man is not so friendly as he should be toward the Feathered Friends and Furry Friends who are his neighbors. And so they have grown to be afraid of him. If we are kind to the little Wild Creatures, they will learn that we are their friends, and then they will trust us.

As I write this, I look out through my workroom window and see Mrs. Ringneck the Pheasant sneaking through the Green Alfalfa in search of a Secret Nesting Place. Burlingame the Meadow Lark is singing his best from the top of a fence post. Robin Red is spying out Wriggly Earthworms on the lawn. Mrs. Bluebird is busy carrying bits of soft grass into her new Nesting Box, while Mr. Bluebird stands guard. Noisy the English Sparrow is scolding because he cannot be in a dozen places at once to bully his neighbors. Down in the swamp Redwing the Blackbird sings "Oak-a-*lee*" from morning till night. And everything tells me that Jolly Spring is here.

How nice it will be in the New Earth, when life will be Eternal Springtime and the Little Creatures will no longer be wild! Then Jack Frost will not destroy the Dancing Little Leaflets and Fragrant Flowers, nor Old Man Winter drive away our Feathered Friends every year; for there will be no such thing as a year.

THE AUTHOR.

Denver, Colorado.

CHAPTER 1

The Arrival of the Mallards

THE morning was chilly, with Gray Cloud Ships blanketing the sky. By noon a heavy mist was falling, which soon turned into Wet Little Raindrops, and as it grew colder Merry Little Snowflakes began to fall.

All day Mr. and Mrs. Mallard and their friends had been flying northward against the storm. They had spent the winter in the warm swamps of Louisiana, and they were returning to their summer home in the Land of Cool Breezes. Ordinarily they would have rested during the storm, but they were anxious to reach a pond which was one of their favorite stopping places on their journeys north and south each spring and fall. There was a Sheltered Little Cove along one side of it where Tumbled Bulrushes and Waving Wild Rice grew, and not far away there were many grainfields, which always contained enough scattered heads of wheat and ears of corn to furnish food in case there was not enough Waving Wild Rice.

Toward evening the wind grew stronger and the falling snow was blinding. Mr. and Mrs. Mallard and their companions were flying low to avoid

Near the Grand Old House was a Duck Pond where
Mr. and Mrs. Mallard felt safe and happy.

the wind as much as possible, and were hoping that they might see a sheltered place where they could spend the night.

Not once during the journey had they encountered Terror the Hunter, with his deadly gun that roared and spat shot at them. They were not much afraid now. You see, Friendly Folk had made laws to stop Terror the Hunter from shooting ducks in the spring; but of course the Mallards did not know that.

Suddenly there was a boom beneath them, and Mr. Mallard felt a stinging pain in one of his wings. He reeled downward for an instant, but caught himself and went on as fast as he could. Mrs. Mallard and their companions had scattered and were soon out of sight in the falling snow. He wondered if any of them had fallen.

Mr. Mallard quacked a signal to Mrs. Mallard as loud as he could. His voice was soft and husky, and he was afraid she would not hear him in the storm. He quacked again, and soon he heard Mrs. Mallard's loud answer.

"Qua-ack quack-quack-quack," she said, and as quickly as possible she flew to his side. "Are you hurt, dear?" she asked.

Mr. Mallard did not want to alarm her, so he pretended that he did not hear. He called reassur-

Sure enough, right ahead of Mr. and Mrs. Mallard, and not more than a block away, was a pond.

ingly in his softest tone of voice, and tried bravely to fly ahead of Mrs. Mallard to break the wind for her. Soon he felt himself growing weaker.

"I wish we could find a place to stop for the night," he said, still trying not to alarm Mrs. Mallard; "the storm seems to be getting worse."

"If we could reach the Duck Pond on the Old Homestead, how nice it would be!" said Mrs. Mallard. "It can't be far away."

They coasted downward to be nearer the ground again, hoping that they could see water on which to alight. Sure enough, right ahead of them, and not more than a block away, was a pond.

"It's the Duck Pond; it is, it is!" quacked Mrs. Mallard excitedly. "How glad I am to see it!"

In a moment they were resting on the surface of

the water in the shelter of the Fuzzy Cattails; and, what is more, they were in the midst of their companions. It was the Favorite Pond toward which they had been flying all day.

By the following morning the sky had cleared, and Mr. Mallard's companions were ready to resume their northward journey, which would carry them perhaps to Canada. Mr. Mallard's wing felt sore and stiff; when he tried to fly, he found that he had not enough strength to leave the water.

"You must go on with the others," he told Mrs. Mallard; "and when I am strong enough, I will follow."

His green head glistened in the morning sunlight, and his colorful wings shone like half rainbows. It was because of his beauty that Terror the Hunter had directed his aim at Mr. Mallard. Always, it seems, Fearful the Man wants the best there is. Mrs. Mallard was as good as Mr. Mallard, but her dress was not quite so pretty. She lacked the green on her head, although it was as trim and smart-looking as Mr. Mallard's. Also, she lacked the bronze on her neck, and she was not quite so colorful in other ways as he.

Mrs. Mallard loved her mate dearly, and she would not agree to any such thing as leaving him behind. No, sir! She felt that her place was right by his side, and she told Mr. Mallard plainly that she expected to stay until he was well enough to leave with her. Of course he was glad to hear her say that, and he did not mind so much when he saw his companions fly away to the northward.

He purred a low farewell to them as they arose from the water, and Mrs. Mallard went a short way with them, quacking loudly that she and Mr. Mallard would soon follow. It happened, however, that by the time Mr. Mallard felt strong enough to fly, they had grown to like the Duck Pond on the Old Homestead so well that they decided to stay for the summer.

That is how Mr. and Mrs. Mallard came to be neighbors of Bud and Mary Smith, when ordinarily they would have been flying far to the northward with many other Mallards, with Honker the Goose, Whitey the Brant, and a host of other Feathered Friends.

CHAPTER 2

The Duck Pond

"I BELIEVE I'll swim around the Duck Pond and see what I can find," said Mrs. Mallard, after their companions had left.

"And I shall go along," said Mr. Mallard.

"Yes, we'll go together," agreed Mrs. Mallard.

You see, although Mr. Mallard's wing was stiff and sore if he tried to fly, yet he could swim without any trouble. So the Mallards set out from among the Fuzzy Cattails and Waving Wild Rice to explore the Duck Pond. Although they had stopped there several times on their journeys, they had never really seen much of the Duck Pond, and they did not know much about the Old Homestead. Usually they stopped in the evening, and by the time the Laughing Yellow Sun was up the next morning, and they had had a good feed of rice, they were ready to leave. Sometimes they flew mostly at night, resting and eating during the day.

Twice each year the Mallards stopped for a feed at the Duck Pond on the Old Homestead. Once was in the fall, when Old Man Winter was coming down from the Land of Ice, and, of course, the Mallards were then usually in a hurry to reach the

Sunny Southland, where they stayed in the swamps and on the rivers. When Jolly Spring began to melt the ice on the lakes and streams, and to chase Old Man Winter back to his home in the Land of Ice, the Mallards were ready to leave the Sunny Southland and return to the Land of Cool Breezes. Then they stopped at the Duck Pond again.

When Mr. and Mrs. Mallard fly from their northern home to the Sunny Southland and then back again in the spring, we say they are migrating. That was what they were doing when Mr. Mallard was shot.

Mrs. Mallard swam to the edge of the Fuzzy Cattails and peeped out. There was still some ice on the Duck Pond in places. It was more than a block wide, and on the distant bank there were many Drooping Willows and other trees. Beyond this fringe of trees and Jungle Thickets was the Green Meadow, and if Mrs. Mallard had been where she could look across it, she would have seen the Grand Old House and the Rambling Old Barn and the Apple Orchard and the rest of the interesting things on the Old Homestead. As it was, all she could see in the distance was High Cliff, which ran along one side of the Old Homestead. You see, Mrs. Mallard was not high enough to look around while she was sitting on the water, for the banks

of the Duck Pond and the trees and the Jungle
Thickets hid everything from sight. And Mrs.
Mallard's neck was not long.

Mr. Mallard swam to her side and peered out
also. Everything seemed quiet and safe. And so
the Mallards swam a little farther. Of course they
did not swim far from shore. Oh, no. They stayed
close to the Fuzzy Cattails along the bank so they
could dive into them and hide if danger came near.
They were not well acquainted around the Old
Homestead, and did not know that Farmer Smith
would not allow Terror the Hunter there with his
gun if he knew it. They did not know that every
little way around the Duck Pond Farmer Smith
had nailed a sign to a tree, which said in big black
letters: "No Hunting Allowed." So they were
watchful.

But Terror the Hunter was not the only one that
the Mallards were watching out for. There was
Sharptoes the Duck Hawk, who might dart down
upon them any time. And even Aquila the Golden
Eagle, whose nest was on a Rocky Pinnacle on the
top of High Cliff, might swoop through the air on
silent wings if they were not watching.

Suddenly a shadow flashed across the water in
front of Mrs. Mallard. For a moment it frightened
her; then she heard the greeting of Mr. Bluebird.

"Good morning," he sang. "Tru-ally, tru-ally, this is a fine morning."

"Qua-ack quack-quack-quack," said Mrs. Mallard, which was her way of saying how glad she was to see Mr. Bluebird. "I suppose you are on your way northward."

"Oh, no," replied Mr. Bluebird; "I am as far north as I am going. You see, Mrs. Bluebird and I live with many Feathered Friends on the Old Homestead during the summer. We had a Hollow Nesting Post by the Apple Orchard and we lived in it three summers. But this spring Bud Smith built a new Nesting Box for us. He put it on an iron pipe in the yard by the Grand Old House. We like it, because Hunting Cat cannot climb up to rob our nest."

"Perhaps you can tell us more about the Old Homestead," said Mr. Mallard. "Terror the Hunter shot my wing, and if it doesn't get better soon, we shall have to stay here."

"Sure-ly, sure-ly I can tell you more," said Mr. Bluebird, and he flew to the top of a Fuzzy Cattail nearer the Mallards. "My nearest neighbor is Robin Red, who lives in the Red Cedar in the yard near us. Then there is Jenny Wren, who expects to build a nest in the eaves of the Grand Old House. She tried to take our Nesting Box, but Judge

Flicker picked out a knot, which made a nice doorway for her in the eaves, and she liked it better than the Nesting Box. Of course Noisy the English Sparrow tried to steal our Nesting Box, but Mrs. Noisy decided she did not like a home without a porch. Bobby White and Woodsy Thrush live in the Hedgerow that runs along the Apple Orchard. Molly Cottontail and Peter live in a Friendly Burrow in the Little Jungle Thicket at the foot of High Cliff, and Johnny Chuck has a Hidden Den under a rock not far from Molly and Peter on the side of High Cliff. I am sure you will like the Old Homestead if you stay. You can go cruising in Little River sometimes, and Bobby White says that Farmer Smith never permits any shooting there."

"And where is Little River?" asked Mrs. Mallard.

"It winds through the Green Meadow and the Wide-Wide Pasture where Old Bent Horn lives," replied Mr. Bluebird. "But I must be going now to see that no one takes the Nesting Box from us."

With that, Mr. Bluebird flew away toward the Grand Old House.

CHAPTER 3

Mrs. Mallard Makes a Discovery

"I'M glad to hear that there is no hunting on the Old Homestead," said Mrs. Mallard, after Mr. Bluebird had left. She felt quite relieved, and quacked loudly as she started again to explore the Duck Pond.

"Qua-ack quack-quack-quack," she said, and flapped her wings against the water. She really made quite a noise, for Bud and Mary Smith heard it away up at the Grand Old House as they were leaving for school.

"I hear some wild ducks on the Duck Pond," exclaimed Bud; "let's go past there and count them."

In a short time they were sneaking through the Jungle Thicket that grew along one side of the pond. At last Bud parted the bushes and looked out.

"There are only two," he whispered as he held up two fingers; "a pair of Mallards."

"I wonder what they are doing here," said Mary. "They must be lost."

"Perhaps one of them is wounded," said Bud.

"Oh, I do wish they would stay," said Mary, as they hurried on to school.

Mr. and Mrs. Mallard did not know that they

had been seen. Mrs. Mallard stood on her head in the water, with her tail pointing straight up, while she reached for a mouthful of Oozy Mud in which she hoped to find some grains of wild rice or a Wriggly Waterworm. Mr. Mallard swam around in wide circles, looking for choice morsels to eat, and with one eye watching for Sharptoes.

At last Mr. Mallard became tired. His wing was sore, and he decided to rest awhile. So he swam to a bunch of Waving Wild Rice and Tumbled Bulrushes and crawled beneath them. He was entirely out of sight and felt quite safe unless Trailer the Mink came along. Mr. Mallard knew that Trailer the Mink seldom came out of his Hidden Den during the day, so he tucked his bill under his strong wing and went to sleep.

Mrs. Mallard was having too good a time to

Mrs. Mallard stood on her head in the water, with her tail pointing straight up.

think about sleeping. She swam here and there, while she explored the Sheltered Water Lanes that wound in and out among the clumps of Swamp Grass and Fuzzy Cattails. Every place she went there was plenty to eat. The more she saw of the Duck Pond, the better she liked it.

Only once did Mrs. Mallard think about going farther northward. That was when a flock of ducks flew over. It was Sawbill the Merganser and some of his friends. Mrs. Mallard quacked loudly to attract his attention. She thought perhaps he might like to stop and rest. But Sawbill the Merganser was not quite ready to stop for that day. You see, he was not much interested in such things as Waving Wild Rice to eat. Sawbill was fond of fish. His bill had sharp points on each side like the teeth of a saw, with which he caught fish, and he ate so many that his flesh was fairly flavored with them. He was like the person who smokes so much that he smells like tobacco smoke. Sawbill the Merganser knew where there was a lake that held many fish, so he hurried on as if he had not heard Mrs. Mallard's invitation to stop.

A little later two more ducks flew over quite low. They were Mr. and Mrs. Spoonbill. Again Mrs. Mallard quacked an invitation to stop. When Shoveler the Spoonbill heard it, he called to Mrs.

Sawbill the Merganser was fond of fish, and his bill had sharp points on each side to help him catch them.

Spoonbill. Then they turned and circled back to the Duck Pond.

"Qua-ack quack-quack-quack," said Mrs. Mallard; "this is a nice place to stop."

Soon Mr. and Mrs. Spoonbill were floating lightly on the water near Mrs. Mallard, and squirting soft mud through the comblike strainers on the sides of their broad bills. Shoveler the Spoonbill had a funny way of eating. First he filled his large, spoonlike bill with Oozy Mud or floating things. Then he strained this mouthful by working water through it. If the strainers held anything in his mouth that he liked after the water had washed away the mud, he swallowed it. Perhaps that was his way of washing his food before he ate it.

(25)

It was not long until Mrs. Mallard and the Spoonbills were good friends, and they swam along together exploring the Duck Pond. Halfway around the Duck Pond they saw a Sheltered Water Lane that seemed to lead into a Sheltered Little Cove. Mrs. Mallard swam into it and looked around. It did not take her long to see that it suited her exactly. On all sides were Fuzzy Cattails, Waving Wild Rice, and Swamp Grass. There was an open space in the center large enough for Fluffy Ducklets to play in, and back from the water was a grassy bank with brush where Mrs. Mallard could build a nest.

Yes, the place suited Mrs. Mallard exactly, and she started back to tell Mr. Mallard about it. She did not wait to swim back, but arose in the air, and in a few moments her strong wings had carried her to the place where she had left Mr. Mallard asleep.

"Qua-ack quack-quack-quack," she called in a loud voice, and soon she heard Mr. Mallard's low voice coming from among the Fuzzy Cattails.

You may be sure it did not take long for her to tell Mr. Mallard about the Sheltered Little Cove. Soon they were swimming back to it, with Mrs. Mallard ahead quacking excitedly.

"I know you will like it; I know you will," she said.

Mrs. Mallard reached the Sheltered Water Lane and turned in, followed closely by Mr. Mallard. They found the Spoonbills still enjoying a feast of the things that grew in the Sheltered Little Cove, and soon Mr. Mallard was acquainted with them also.

"I believe we'll stay right here this summer," said Mrs. Mallard.

"I think we shall, too," said Mrs. Spoonbill.

That is how the Mallards and the Spoonbills happened to be neighbors at the Duck Pond on the Old Homestead.

CHAPTER 4

Redwing the Blackbird Moves In

REDWING the Blackbird was a jolly fellow. In the fall he had joined a large flock of his gentlemen friends, and they had played and had sung together all winter. They had flown from place to place, sometimes here and sometimes there, as if they had not a care in the world and nothing to do but to travel. They enjoyed seeing new places. Usually they selected a swamp for their stopping place, where there were plenty of Fuzzy Cattails and Tumbled Bulrushes for them to perch on.

Mrs. Blackbird and the other lady Blackbirds had gone south, but Redwing and his friends were never in a hurry to leave in the fall. They were never in a hurry to go anywhere, for that matter. If the weather was not too severe, they sometimes stayed in the Chilly Northland until Merry Little Snowflakes lay so deep upon the weeds that Redwing could find little to eat. Then he and his friends would fly away toward the Sunny Southland for a while, but they were likely to return to the Chilly Northland with the first hint of fair weather.

Redwing and his friends had been playing together for months, flying from place to place. One day after Mrs. Blackbird arrived, they spied a Sheltered Little Cove on the edge of a small lake, where Fuzzy Cattails and Swamp Grasses were plentiful. Of course they stopped to investigate, and the place suited Redwing and a few of his friends so well they decided to stay.

Not that Redwing and Mrs. Blackbird were ready to start nest building then. Oh, no. Redwing was never in a hurry to build a nest any more than he was in a hurry to do anything else. Sometimes it was June before Mrs. Blackbird built her nest, and even then Redwing was not much help with the family work. Perhaps the reason that Mrs. Blackbird did not build a nest sooner was that she was waiting for the new Fuzzy Cattails to grow larger.

You see, Mrs. Blackbird liked to build her nest over the water, and usually she used the Fuzzy Cattails in which to build it. Perhaps she waited until the new ones were high enough for shelter. It would be hard to say why Mrs. Blackbird chose to build her nest over water, for it certainly seemed as if that was a dangerous place for Wee Blackbirds to live. What if one of them should have fallen out of the nest?

It may have been that Mrs. Blackbird was vain, and liked to build her nest where she could see her reflection in the water. More than likely she built it there so Hunting Cat and other prowlers could not get to it, for Mrs. Blackbird really had little to be vain about as far as looks were concerned. Her streaked brown coat was very common-looking indeed, and she could not sing. She did not have the shiny black coat and flashy red wing patches that Redwing had. It is no wonder he liked to spread his wings when he sang and to display the scarlet marks that looked very much like the stripes on a soldier's coat sleeve.

No, it was not yet time for the Blackbirds to start housekeeping; so they flitted from one Fuzzy Cattail to another and explored their new home. That is what they were doing when they met the

"Oak-a-lee," sang Redwing the Blackbird, when he first met the Mallards, which was his way of saying: "Hello there, neighbors."

Mallards, for of course the Sheltered Little Cove that Redwing had found was the same one where the Mallards were living at the Duck Pond.

"Oak-a-*lee*," sang Redwing the Blackbird, when he first met the Mallards. That was his way of saying: "Hello there, neighbors."

"Qua-ack quack-quack-quack," said Mrs. Mallard, and right away they both knew they would be good friends.

"How long do you plan to stay here?" asked Redwing, for he was not expecting that the Mallards would stay all summer.

"Oh, we are living here now," replied Mrs. Mallard. "You see, Greenhead was shot through the wing and could go no farther." "Greenhead" was Mrs. Mallard's favorite name for Mr. Mallard.

"Then we shall be neighbors all summer," said Redwing, "for I expect to live in the Sheltered Little Cove."

"Yes, and have you met Shoveler and Mrs. Spoonbill?" asked Mrs. Mallard. "They will be our neighbors also. They have gone over to explore Little River today."

"I have not seen them," said Redwing; "but I shall be glad to meet them."

"Perhaps you would find them if you flew over to Little River," said Mrs. Mallard.

Shoveler and Mrs Spoonbill were glad to see the Mallards and to know that they were to be neighbors during the summer.

"I believe I will," replied Redwing, and away he and Mrs. Blackbird flew.

Redwing liked Little River almost as well as he liked the Sheltered Little Cove. He found Jungle Thickets and tall grass and rushes in places growing along its banks. There were Quiet Pools where the water flowed slowly past Broad Bends, and it was in one of these that Redwing found the Spoonbills. They were enjoying a feast of good things that they found along the bank.

"Oak-a-*lee*," sang Redwing the Blackbird.

"Chack-chack," said Mrs. Blackbird.

Of course the Spoonbills were glad to see them and to hear that they were to be neighbors during the summer.

"I am sure that we shall get along nicely," said Shoveler. "Mrs. Mallard said that Mr. Bluebird told her that Bobby White told him that Farmer Smith did not permit hunting on the Old Homestead. And so we should not be disturbed."

As Shoveler said that, there was a terrific noise over at the Duck Pond. There could be no mistake about it; it was the sound of a gun. It roared across the little valley, and its echo came back from the side of High Cliff.

"Oh, dear," said Mrs. Spoonbill, "I do hope that the Mallards were not killed. I wish we could go to see if they are safe."

"I see someone running across the Green Meadow from the Grand Old House," said Redwing, from his High Perch on a Drooping Willow Tree. "It must be Farmer Smith."

"I hope he catches Terror the Hunter," said Shoveler.

It was a long time before the Spoonbills and the Blackbirds ventured back to the Duck Pond.

CHAPTER 5

Terror the Hunter Makes a Mistake

PERHAPS you would like to know more about Terror the Hunter. He lived in a Low Yellow House by the railroad tracks and worked for the railroad. He was called a "section hand." He was not a citizen of our country and could not read our language. So he knew nothing about the game laws, or, if he did, he did not care.

Terror the Hunter owned a gun. It was against the law for a foreigner to own a gun, but he did not care about that, either. When he went hunting, he killed any of the little Wild Creatures that he could find. He would as soon shoot Burlingame the Meadow Lark and other songbirds as anything. He was the greatest enemy that the Feathered Friends and Furry Friends knew.

Whenever word went out among the little Wild Creatures that Terror the Hunter was afield all of them tried to hide because of fear that he might find them.

One day when Terror the Hunter was not working he took down his gun and started out with a pocket full of ammunition. He was not quite sure where to go, but he thought he might

(34)

If Terror the Hunter could have read the sign nailed to a tree, it would have warned him not to hunt there.

find something to shoot. He was not at all particular about what he killed or ate.

After a while he saw a pond. He thought there might be ducks on it, or blackbirds in the rushes along its edge. It was the Duck Pond on the Old Homestead; but Terror the Hunter did not know that. He crept across a field until he came to the Drooping Willow Trees and Jungle Thickets near the Duck Pond. He saw a board with some letters on it, that was nailed to a tree, but he could not read it. If he could have, it would have warned him not to hunt there.

Terror the Hunter crawled under the fence and into the Jungle Thicket. Carefully he sneaked through the brush, for he did not wish to make a noise by breaking any of the Dry Sticks. That

(35)

would have told the little Wild Creatures that danger was near, and that was the last thing Terror the Hunter wanted them to know.

At last Terror the Hunter reached the edge of the Duck Pond. He parted the Tumbled Bulrushes and looked out. There on the water near the center of the Duck Pond was a gray duck that looked like Mrs. Mallard from a distance. It was a little too far away to shoot, so Terror settled down in his Hiding Place and waited. He thought that the duck would swim nearer to him if he stayed out of sight and waited.

The gray duck was having a fine time. It swam here and there in search of good things to eat, and really did not seem as if it were paying much attention to anything around it.

At last the gray duck began to swim toward Terror the Hunter. Of course Terror was glad. He thought he would have a fine fat duck to eat. He expected to shoot the duck and wait for the Playful Air Whiffs to blow it to shore so he could get it.

When the duck was near enough, Terror the Hunter raised his gun and fired. He was sure he would see a dead duck lying on the water. But that was one time Terror was mistaken. Instead of seeing a dead duck, he did not see any duck at all.

You see, the gray duck was not Mrs. Mallard. It was Diver the Grebe.

Diver the Grebe was an active duck. He could dive faster than you could wink your eye. He did not like to fly; so, whenever danger came near, he would dive out of sight. Then he would swim under water and come up a long way from the place where he went under. Diver the Grebe could dive so swiftly that he was under the water before Terror the Hunter's shot got to him.

A little later he came up away out in the middle of the Duck Pond. That was too far for Terror the Hunter to shoot, and Diver the Grebe knew it. He knew he was safe, and he went ahead with his feeding as if nothing had happened.

Of course Terror the Hunter was disappointed.

The gray duck was not Mrs. Mallard. It was Diver the Grebe.

He did not know that Mr. and Mrs. Mallard were hiding on the other side of the Duck Pond. They swam into some Tumbled Bulrushes out of sight. They could not quite understand why it was that Terror the Hunter was shooting on the Duck Pond when Mr. Bluebird had said that Bobby White had told him that Farmer Smith did not allow hunting. They were not quite sure that they liked the Duck Pond as well as they had. They hid in the Tumbled Bulrushes to talk it over. They did not know that right then Farmer Smith was hurrying across the Green Meadow to catch Terror the Hunter.

Farmer Smith was a deputy game warden. That is, he was asked by the state to protect the little Wild Creatures from Terror the Hunter. Farmer Smith was glad to do this because he knew the little Wild Creatures were his friends, and he liked them. Sometimes the state brought Feathered Friends like Hungarian the Partridge from distant countries and turned them loose on the Old Homestead. Then Farmer Smith protected them from Terror the Hunter.

You may be sure that Terror the Hunter was surprised when Farmer Smith stepped out of the brush and grabbed him. That was the last time Terror came to the Old Homestead to hunt. He had to give up his gun and pay a fine for hunting on posted land out of season without a license. That taught Terror a lesson he never forgot.

The Mallards did not know all this, but they did know that Farmer Smith had taken Terror away, because Redwing the Blackbird told them so. He had seen the whole thing from his High Perch on a Drooping Willow Tree.

Of course when the Mallards and the Spoonbills and the other little Wild Creatures heard that Farmer Smith had taken Terror away, they were all glad.

"Oak-a-*lee*," sang Redwing the Blackbird.

CHAPTER 6

Longlegs the Heron Goes Wading

CROAKER the Frog sat on a pile of dead Swamp Grass at the edge of the Duck Pond singing. At least he probably called it "singing." But it was a very different song from the one that Redwing the Blackbird was singing not far away. Croaker's voice was coarse and harsh. It sounded about like a stone rolling around in an empty tin can.

But Croaker the Frog was happy, and even though he could not sing so sweetly as Redwing and some of the Feathered Friends, still he was doing the best he could. No doubt it sounded beautiful to him, and Croaker should not be blamed for doing his best any more than we would want to be if we were working or singing or doing something else as well as we could.

Croaker had hatched from an egg the summer before. At first he was a Wriggly Tadpole that looked like a big head with a tail fastened to it. Croaker could swim quite well with his tail, but it was not long until he started to grow legs. His hind legs started to grow first, and then his front ones came into sight. Of course, his hind legs were

(40)

Croaker the Frog was happy, and though he could not
sing so sweetly as some of his Feathered Friends,
still he was doing the best he could.

much the larger because he needed them with
which to hop and swim. As his legs grew larger,
his tail grew smaller, until it disappeared entirely.
He did not need it when he had legs. It would
have been in his way when he hopped. The Creator knew this when He made Croaker, and we can
frequently see God's wisdom shown in other ways
in nature if we will but look for it.

Croaker the Frog had been asleep all winter.
When the ice began to freeze on the Duck Pond the
fall before and Croaker could no longer swim about
from place to place, he burrowed down into the
Oozy Mud, and there he stayed until Jolly Spring
came and melted the ice. Then he crawled out
from his muddy bed, kicked his legs a few times

to limber them up, and climbed out into the Bright Little Sunbeams.

The Laughing Yellow Sun warmed Croaker's back and made him happy. Now and then an early fly or other insect came close enough for him to catch. Sometimes he found insects floating on the water. It all made Croaker happy, so he tried his best to tell others about it. He croaked as loud as he could, and each time he croaked he puffed out a large sac under his chin.

When listening to Croaker the Frog, one might have thought that he did not have any worries at all. But Croaker did have troubles the same as everyone. One of the things that bothered him was Longlegs the Heron. Right then when Croaker was singing his solo, Longlegs the Heron was out looking for him.

Longlegs had been wading along Little River. He liked to wade along its banks in search of minnows and frogs. Longlegs had not been very successful that day. It was a little too early for frogs in Little River. Then, when he was getting ready to fly back to his perch in a Giant Cottonwood, he heard a croak. It sounded as though it came from the Duck Pond.

"Aha," thought Longlegs, "Croaker the Frog is out at last. I believe I'll fly over to the Duck

Pond and go wading there for a while. I surely would like a frog for supper."

Longlegs had eaten many minnows that day. They were plentiful in Little River. But he could not seem to find any frogs. Longlegs was fond of frogs. He would stalk along the bank of the Duck Pond among the rushes and water lilies for hours looking for frogs. Croaker the Frog and his friends were not so easy to catch. Their backs were the color of the green things on which they sat, and it took sharp eyes to see them.

Did you ever notice that a frog's eyes are set right on top of its head? That is another wise provision that the Creator made for Croaker and his friends. You see, when Croaker's eyes were on top like that, he could sit with all of his body under water. Only his eyes and nose stuck out. In that way he could find a Hiding Place in the water under a large leaf or bunch of water grass. Sometimes he would sit quietly and wait until a fly or mosquito almost lit on his nose. That would be the end of Mr. Mosquito.

With his eyes sticking out on top of his head, Croaker could watch in every direction for danger. If Longlegs the Heron came near, Croaker would take a full breath of air and settle quietly to the bottom of the Duck Pond among the grass roots.

But Longlegs was a skillful hunter. He was quiet, and he had sharp eyes. Sometimes Croaker's friends were so interested with their singing that they forgot to watch for Longlegs. Before they knew it, Longlegs would straighten the bends in his long neck with one swift thrust, and down the red lane they would go.

Longlegs lit in the water near the bank of the Duck Pond and started wading. First he raised one foot carefully, and then with his toes still held together so they would not make a noise, he stepped ahead. Then he drew up the other foot and held it a moment before stepping ahead.

It is impossible to say whether or not Longlegs would have caught Croaker if nothing had interfered. But as Longlegs was nearing the place where Croaker was sitting on his bunch of Swamp Grass singing, along came Lutra the Otter, who went kerplunk into the water.

That spoiled everything for Longlegs the Heron. Croaker did not know who had made such a splash, but he knew it was time to dive out of sight. Croaker dove into the water so quickly he hardly had time to take a full breath of air first. And Longlegs the Heron decided he would have to wait until another day to catch Croaker.

CHAPTER 7

Lutra the Otter Plays a Game

OF course Lutra the Otter had no idea that he had alarmed Croaker the Frog. He did not even know that Croaker was there.

Lutra the Otter was a near relative of Trailer the Mink, Snoop the Weasel, and Killer the Marten. He lived in a Friendly Burrow among the spreading roots of a Giant Cottonwood that stood on the bank of Little River. The doorway to his home was under water, and you never would have noticed it, if you didn't already know where it was.

Lutra spent most of his time fishing. He would catch fish and kill them for fun whether he was hungry or not. He was like some people who take more on their plate than they can eat, and then waste it. Lutra had great sport while he was catching the fish, but the one who wastes food has no excuse whatever.

One reason why Lutra the Otter was such an expert fisherman was that he was so active in water. He had webs between his toes like a duck, which enabled him to swim swiftly through the water; and the end of his tail was flattened like a rudder, which he used for turning himself quickly. Lutra

Lutra the Otter spent
most of his time fish-
ing. He would catch
fish for fun, whether he was hungry or not.

could stay under water for a long time when he
was after fish.

In some countries people have trained Lutra's
friends to fish for them. They send the trained
otters into the water, and when an otter has caught
a fish, he brings it to his master as a trained dog
will fetch game.

Lutra the Otter was a great traveler. Sometimes
he would be gone from his Friendly Burrow almost
two weeks. Usually he traveled with several of his
friends. They would visit a number of places along
Little River, then cross over to another stream and
follow down it a way, and on their way back they
would stop awhile at the Duck Pond.

It is strange how Lutra the Otter could travel so
far without becoming lost. But he always found

his way back to his Friendly Burrow among the spreading roots of the Giant Cottonwood. That was one of his secrets.

"Let us visit the Black Forest," said Lutra the Otter to his friends one day.

The Black Forest was one place that Lutra liked to visit. It was there that Paddletail the Beaver had built a High Dam and made himself a Wildwood Pond. And the Wildwood Pond held many, many fish. Paddletail the Beaver did not care if Lutra and his friends caught fish in his Wildwood Pond. Paddletail did not eat fish, and so he had no use for them. Paddletail ate the Soft Poplar Wood and Bitter Willow Bark that grew near his Wildwood Pond.

Lutra the Otter and his friends started out to visit Paddletail's Wildwood Pond. They followed along Little River for quite a distance, because Little River flowed through the Black Forest before it arrived at the Old Homestead. It was Little River that Paddletail the Beaver had dammed to make his Wildwood Pond. Little River was not large away up in the Black Forest where Paddletail lived. It had not had time to grow. In fact, it was not large when it reached the Old Homestead. But it was a jolly, playful, singing Little River nevertheless.

Lutra the Otter and his friends were not in a hurry to reach Paddletail's Wildwood Pond in the Black Forest. Oh, no. They liked to play too well for that. Besides seeing who could catch the most fish, they had another game that they played. It was the game of Slide.

If you like to coast downhill, you know how much fun Lutra and his friends had sliding. But Lutra did not need snow when he went sliding. He would find a steep bank that sloped downward to a Deep Pool. Then, while his smooth fur was wet, he would run to the top of the bank and coast down on his stomach kerplunk into the water. Right behind him was one of his friends, and soon another would follow. Then Lutra would be back for another slide.

Kerplunk, kerplunk, kerplunk. Soon the Mud Slide would be wet and slick, and they could coast faster and faster. It really was great sport. Lutra and his friends had made a Mud Slide whenever they could find a suitable place along Little River, and whenever they came to a Mud Slide they stopped to play awhile. Kerplunk, kerplunk, kerplunk. Sometimes Lutra came up with a fish in his mouth.

At last Lutra the Otter and his friends reached Paddletail's Wildwood Pond. They had built an extra long Mud Slide there. You should have seen how fast they could shoot down it into the water.

Paddletail the Beaver was out repairing his High Dam when he heard a splash. Soon there was another and another. Kerplunk, kerplunk, kerplunk.

"Lutra the Otter and his friends must be here again," said Paddletail.

After they had coasted awhile and had fished until they were tired, Lutra and his friends crawled into a Hiding Place and went to sleep. Then they awoke and started back toward the Friendly Burrow among the spreading roots of the Giant Cottonwood that stood on the bank of Little River on the Old Homestead.

"Let's go back past the Duck Pond," said Lutra to his friends. So they did.

Paddletail the Beaver was out repairing his High Dam when he heard a splash.

4—M

The first thing Lutra did when he arrived at the Duck Pond was to dive kerplunk into the water. That is how he happened to make such a splash right by Croaker the Frog in time to frighten Croaker away before Longlegs the Heron caught him.

Of course it would not have made any difference to Lutra the Otter even though he had seen that Longlegs wanted to catch Croaker, for Lutra was having too much fun to care.

Kerplunk, kerplunk, kerplunk went Lutra and his friends.

CHAPTER 8

Mr. Mallard Flies Again

IT had been three weeks since Mr. and Mrs. Mallard had arrived at the Duck Pond on the Old Homestead. Of course Mr. Mallard had not been able to fly with his wounded wing. He had had to be contented to swim around the Duck Pond. So he had not been over to Little River, and he had not seen much of the Old Homestead.

Mrs. Mallard had not gone far from the Duck Pond either, because she had wanted to stay near Mr. Mallard. They had lived most of the time in the Sheltered Little Cove.

One day Mr. Mallard saw Great Diver the Loon fishing on the other side of the Duck Pond. He wondered if he dared attempt to fly over for a visit with Great Diver.

Mr. Mallard spread his wings and fluttered them swiftly. His wounded wing seemed to be all right. He ran along on the water for a way while he flapped his wings faster and faster. Soon he was in the air, and Mrs. Mallard was surprised to see him flying across the Duck Pond to see Great Diver the Loon.

Mr. Mallard was quite out of breath when he

alighted on the water near Great Diver, but he managed to purr a low greeting with his coarse voice.

Great Diver the Loon was a large cousin of Diver the Grebe. He was almost as large as Honker the Goose. He could dive about as well as Diver the Grebe. When he was on land, he did not stand on his feet as most of his Feathered Friends did. He sort of sat up straight on his stubby tail and rested with his legs as well as his feet on the ground. That made him look dignified.

Great Diver liked to fish. He could dive under the water and swim long distances before he came up again. Or, if he wished, he could swim with only his head showing. That was one secret that Mr. Mallard did not know, but Diver the Grebe had also learned it.

Great Diver the Loon was a large cousin of Diver the Grebe and was almost as large as Honker the Goose.

Have you ever read about a submarine boat that travels entirely under water when the captain wants it to? To submerge, certain compartments are filled with water. That makes the boat heavy so it will sink. When the water is forced out, the boat rises to the surface of the water again.

Great Diver the Loon had learned that secret, but he knew it better than did Fearful the Man. When he wanted to settle under the water, he emptied the air out of his lungs, and down he sank without diving. He did not even have to stop to fill himself with water in order to become heavy.

Great Diver was fishing when Mr. Mallard arrived. It was the first time he had visited the Duck Pond, but he seemed to be enjoying himself. He had caught a fine fish.

"Do you plan on staying at the Duck Pond this summer?" purred Mr. Mallard.

"Oh, no," replied Great Diver; "I stopped here only to rest and catch some fish. You see, I am afraid Mrs. Loon would think the Duck Pond too small. With Lutra the Otter and Alcyon the Kingfisher and Bigmouth the Pelican and Osprey the Fish Hawk and others all catching fish, it might be hard to feed two babies. We shall find a Nesting Place on a large lake farther north where fish are more plentiful."

Mrs. Loon had a queer way of building her nest. First she bent over some Tumbled Bulrushes until they touched the water. Then she piled other rushes and Swamp Grass on these until she had enough on which to lay her eggs. If the water came higher, her nest floated and rose with the water. If the water lowered, her nest went down also.

Once Mrs. Loon was not careful enough. She did not fasten her nest well enough to the rushes. When a stray wind blew, her nest broke loose from its moorings and went floating across the lake with Mrs. Loon on it.

It is hard to say how long Mr. Mallard and Great Diver would have visited if they had not been disturbed. But Sharptoes the Duck Hawk had spied Mr. Mallard, and said he to himself: "Ah, tonight I shall enjoy a fine duck supper!"

Sharptoes was a wise bird. He flew around behind the Drooping Willow Trees where Mr. Mallard could not see him. Then, when Mr. Mallard and Great Diver were not looking, he sailed out of the trees and swooped down upon them.

But there was one who had seen Sharptoes the Duck Hawk. It was Boomer the Bittern. Boomer had been hiding in the Swamp Grass. He was standing quietly in the water, with his beak pointed almost straight up, waiting for Croaker the Frog or Forktongue the Snake to pass close by. Then he would have grabbed them.

When he saw Sharptoes the Duck Hawk sail over, he knew that Sharptoes was up to mischief. He knew that Sharptoes was after one of the Mallards or the Spoonbills or Midget the Teal. Boomer thought he would warn them.

When Mr. Mallard and Great Diver heard a long b-o-o-m, they immediately dived out of sight under the water, and Sharptoes the Duck Hawk had to look elsewhere for a supper.

Of course, the long b-o-o-m came from Boomer the Bittern. It sounded much as if he had his head under water and was blowing out his breath through a bass horn. Boomer made such a queer noise that Bud and Mary Smith called him "thunder pump."

After Sharptoes had gone, Mr. Mallard flew back to Mrs. Mallard in the Sheltered Little Cove, and Great Diver left the Duck Pond. His wings were rather small, so he had to run on the water to gain speed before taking to the air; but he was soon on his way to the Land of Cool Breezes.

CHAPTER 9

Trailer the Mink Takes a Hunt

TRAILER the Mink was hungry. He had been sleeping all day in his Hidden Den near the Bank of Little River. His Hidden Den was not far from the home of his big cousin Lutra the Otter. Trailer was different from Lutra in several ways. He liked to live near Little River, but he did not like to play in the water so well as Lutra did. Also, he preferred to eat birds, while Lutra liked to eat fish. Trailer the Mink was fond of fish also, but he found it easier to catch birds. Sometimes he found fish that Lutra had killed for the fun of fishing, and then Trailer had a feast. He always enjoyed eating someone else's catch.

It was not yet dark when Trailer came out of his Hidden Den and looked around. Trailer was deciding where he would go.

"I believe I'll go over by the Duck Pond and see what I can find," he said to himself.

Trailer knew that along the Duck Pond there were many Fuzzy Cattails and Tumbled Bulrushes and much Swamp Grass. He also knew that along the Marshy Banks was the favorite haunt of Jack Snipe, Sicklebill the Curlew, and Longbill the

Trailer the Mink was hungry, for he had been sleeping all day in his Hidden Den near the Bank of Little River.

Rail. It was Trailer's Favorite Hunting Ground.

Trailer sat by his Hidden Den and listened. He wondered if it was dark enough so that he would dare to start.

"Cur-lew, cur-lew," said Sicklebill the Curlew over near the Duck Pond. He was proud of his name, and kept repeating it.

"Scaipe, scaipe," said Jack Snipe.

That was too tempting for Trailer the Mink. He left his Hidden Den and started through the grass and brush toward the Duck Pond where he heard Sicklebill the Curlew and Jack Snipe.

It was not strange that Sicklebill and Jack both liked the Marshy Banks along the Duck Pond, because they were near relatives. They were also related to Killdeer the Plover and Sharpnose the Woodcock. One would have thought that Long-bill the Rail was also one of their cousins, because he was small and had a long, pointed bill. Instead, Longbill was a cousin of Sandhill the Crane.

It seems queer that Longbill the Rail, who was not more than half as large as Bobby White, could be related to Sandhill the Crane, who was almost as tall as Bud Smith. But that is true, nevertheless. Longbill had long toes as well as a long bill, and these enabled him to run across muddy ground without sinking. His big cousin, Sandhill the Crane, did not always stay near swamps, but many times lived far from water on the Broad Prairie.

There was one thing about Sicklebill the Curlew that was different from his cousin Jack Snipe. Whenever he alighted on the ground, he always held his wings up in the air for a while, and then deliberately folded them, as if he were quite particular how it was done.

"Cur-lew, cur-lew," called Sicklebill from the Swampy Bank.

When Trailer the Mink left his Hidden Den and started through the grass and brush, he did not go far until he smelled the track of Jimmy the Swamp Rabbit. It smelled fresh, so Trailer slipped noiselessly through the weeds and grass, following Jimmy's trail, thinking he might surprise him.

You see, Trailer had a keen nose. He could not see Jimmy's tracks in the grass, but he could smell them. Trailer had soft feet, for they were padded with hair. If Jimmy did not see him coming, Trailer would have him by the throat before he knew an enemy was near.

After a while Jimmy's trail came back to Little River. That was as far as Trailer could follow him, because Jimmy had swum right across, and had not left any scent for Trailer to follow. Trailer decided he was thirsty, and jumped into Little River for a drink and a bath. Before he came out he found a crawfish. Trailer rather liked crawfish, but one crawfish was not enough to satisfy Trailer's ravenous appetite.

"Cur-lew, cur-lew," called Sicklebill from the Swampy Bank.

"Scaipe, scaipe," answered Jack Snipe.

Away went Trailer the Mink again to see if he could find one of them for supper. Trailer's black eyes looked sharply here and there. Every little

Jack Snipe liked the Marshy
Banks along the Duck Pond.
He was a cousin
of Sicklebill
the Curlew.

way he stopped and sniffed to see if the Playful Air
Whiffs were bringing him the odor of supper.
Then he would slip quietly through the Swamp
Grass and Waving Wild Rice for a while, and
then stop and sniff again.

Suddenly Trailer the Mink stopped and sat up.
He was not far from the edge of he Duck Pond.
He sniffed again to make sure that he had not been
mistaken.

"I smell duck," he said to himself. "My, how
good fat duck will taste!"

Trailer slipped through the grass to the bank
of the pond, and there, only a few feet away sat
Midget the Teal busily engaged in oiling his
feathers. You see, Midget carried a small oil holder
like a pimple on the top of his tail. Before he went
into the water he first rubbed his bill on the oil

holder and then on his feathers. In that way he kept them from getting wet.

Trailer crept a little nearer and made ready to spring. He was lying so flat in the grass that Midget did not see him.

As Trailer was ready to spring on Midget the Teal, there was a loud noise overhead. "Zoom!" went Zoomer the Nighthawk, as he shot down through the air. Of course Midget looked up to see what was going on, and saw Trailer. You may be sure Midget did not wait to finish oiling his feathers.

CHAPTER 10

Mrs. Mallard Builds a Nest

"WHERE are you going?" asked Mr. Mallard one day, as Mrs. Mallard left the Duck Pond and started walking into the dense Swamp Grass and Fuzzy Cattails along their Sheltered Little Cove.

"I am going to look for a Nesting Place," replied Mrs. Mallard. "I heard Mrs. Spoonbill tell Shoveler yesterday that she had already found a place that suited her." Away sneaked Mrs. Mallard as quietly as possible, for she did not want any of the other little Wild Creatures to see her and discover where her Nesting Place would be.

You see, Mrs. Mallard has to be careful where she builds her nest. She must keep it hidden from Billy Coon and Trailer the Mink and Snoop the Weasel and Reddy Fox and many other enemies. Mrs. Mallard cannot build her nest in a tree where Reddy Fox could not get to it, because her feet were not made for roosting in trees.

So Mrs. Mallard was looking for a place on the ground where Trailer the Mink and Billy Coon and Reddy Fox were not likely to go. That was quite a problem for Mrs. Mallard, because there

Mrs. Wood Duck found a Hollow Nesting Tree not far from water.

are few places that are safe from the keen noses of Reddy Fox and Trailer the Mink.

Now, if Mrs. Mallard had been like her cousin Mrs. Wood Duck, it would have been quite easy to build a nest where not even Billy Coon could get to it. That is, it would have been easy if a suitable Hollow Nesting Tree could have been found. Mrs. Wood Duck finds a Hollow Nesting Tree not far from water. If it has a small doorway, then Billy Coon cannot get in and take the Fluffy Ducklets when they are hatched.

How do you suppose the Fluffy Ducklets get out of that hole and to the water before they can fly? First Mrs. Wood Duck takes a Fluffy Ducklet in her bill and flies to the water with it. She leaves it in a Hiding Place and flies back after another and another and another. Soon all of her Fluffy Duck-

(63)

lets are enjoying their first swim, and whenever Mrs. Wood Duck sounds a note of warning, all of the Fluffy Ducklets scamper to a Hiding Place.

Mrs. Mallard did not know this secret. She always built her nest on the ground. But Mrs. Mallard had some secrets of her own, which no doubt were as good as Mrs. Wood Duck's. One of them was to cover herself with old leaves while she was sitting on her eggs. Mrs. Mallard's dress was a grayish-brown striped with black, and when she covered herself with dead leaves and grass, with only her head sticking out, she looked like a pile of trash.

So Mrs. Mallard was quite particular where she built her nest. Once she found a place that suited her exactly, but the color did not match her own. Already the grass was getting green, and there was too much contrast between it and her brown dress.

At last Mrs. Mallard found the place she was looking for. It was between two roots of a Drooping Willow Tree, and was entirely hidden by vines and brush. The ground was covered with the leaves that had fallen the previous fall, and these would make a natural blanket for her. The doorway was between two bushes that hid the Nesting Place from the front, and the big trunk of the

Drooping Willow Tree itself would be a protection from the back. The Nesting Place was near enough to the Sheltered Little Cove so that Mrs. Mallard could run down for a drink and a swim sometimes.

It was not much trouble for Mrs. Mallard to build her nest after she had once found a Nesting Place, and especially when everything was so handy. First she hollowed out a low place between the two roots which formed the sides of her nest. Then she carried some fine grass and Fuzzy Cattail tops and made a nest in the hollow place. After that she plucked some Soft Warm Down from her own breast and lined the nest so the Fluffy Ducklets would not get cold after they were hatched.

Mrs. Mallard was pleased with her nest, and one

Shoveler the Spoonbill was also alone, and sometimes he and Mr. Mallard met for a visit.

day she took Mr. Mallard to see it. Already it held four eggs that looked as if they had been stained a yellow-drab color. Of course Mrs. Mallard kept them mostly hidden with leaves when she was away; but even if she had not, they were so near the color of the leaves they were hard to see.

Within a few more days Mrs. Mallard had a nestful of eggs, and she decided it was time to stay on her nest and keep the eggs warm so that every one would be a Fluffy Ducklet. That left Mr. Mallard alone most of the time when he was not hiding near Mrs. Mallard to watch for enemies. Shoveler the Spoonbill was also alone, and sometimes he and Mr. Mallard met for a visit.

One day Bud and Mary Smith went to the Duck Pond for a walk. They noticed that Mr. Mallard and Shoveler were alone.

"I wonder if Mrs. Mallard and Mrs. Spoonbill are on their nests, or if something has caught them," said Mary.

"My guess would be that they are staying on their nests," said Bud. "It isn't likely that something would catch both of them. That would be quite unusual."

"Oh, I can hardly wait to see the Fluffy Ducklets," said Mary. "I wonder how many the Mallards will have."

After that Bud and Mary each made frequent trips to the Duck Pond when the other wasn't watching. Each wanted to be the first to see the Fluffy Ducklets and tell the other about it.

Mrs. Mallard was so interested and busy with her own affairs that she knew nothing about Mary's and Bud's interest in her Fluffy Ducklets. She was expecting her yellow-drab eggs to hatch almost any time, and she wanted to be near to care for the Fluffy Ducklets when they broke open the shells and came out. She knew that if she did not keep them covered, an enemy might see them.

CHAPTER 11

A Night Prowler

VIRGINIA OPOSSUM lived in a Warm Hollow Log in the Woodlot that joined the Wide-Wide Pasture on the Old Homestead. Virginia had lived there two years. Her nearest neighbor was Worker the Gray Squirrel, who lived in a Big Stick Nest in the top of a tree not far away. His cousin, Chatterer the Red Squirrel, lived in a Hollow Den Tree in the Wide-Wide Pasture, but Worker and Chatterer were not at all friendly.

Virginia Opossum was not much interested in her neighboors. Sometimes Chatterer the Red Squirrel poked his head into Virginia's Warm Hollow Log to see if Worker the Gray Squirrel had stored any nuts there that he could steal. But when he saw Virginia's pink mouth greeting him wide open, with its rows of needlelike teeth, Chatterer went on about his business scolding.

Bud Smith knew where Virginia lived, but he did not disturb her. He had found her home one day while he was in the Woodlot with Nero the Hound. Nero would sniff in every Friendly Burrow and Warm Hollow Log that they passed. Then he would run and catch up with Bud and follow along behind until they passed another Friendly Burrow or Warm Hollow Log.

Once when Nero was walking behind Bud, he stopped suddenly and put his nose to the ground. Then he ran off across the Woodlot barking loudly for Bud to follow. You see, Virginia had passed by on her way home the night before, and Nero's keen nose led him right to her Warm Hollow Log. When Bud looked in, there was Virginia sound asleep. Or it might have been that she was pretending she was dead. Bud called it "playing 'possum."

You see, Virginia had a queer habit of playing dead whenever she was in danger. Perhaps that was why Nero the Hound was so anxious to catch her this time. Once he had surprised her at night on one of her journeys to the cornfield. He had grabbed her by the back with his mouth and car-

Virginia Opossum lived in a Warm Hollow Log in the Woodlot that joined the Wide-Wide Pasture on the Old Homestead.

ried her away. He had thought Virginia was dead. So when he saw Ranger the Coyote running across the Green Meadow, he dropped Virginia and started after him. He thought he would come back after Virginia later. As soon as Nero was out of sight, Virginia suddenly came back to life and ran away; and when Nero returned, there was no Virginia in sight.

That was why Nero was so glad when he found Virginia's home; but Bud called him away, and let Virginia sleep. It seemed she was always sleepy. Perhaps it was because she spent most of the night walking through the Woodlot in search of soft-shelled nuts and wild berries to eat, or rambling about in the cornfield looking for a roasting ear if it was the right time of year, or hoping to find Tiny the Meadow Mouse. Virginia was not at all particular about what she ate as long as it was something she could chew. Sometimes she ate insects, and if she could not find anything else, she ate the tender roots and bulbs of plants that grew in the Woodlot.

One evening about dusk Virginia decided she would go for a walk over by the Duck Pond. She had eleven babies, but that did not worry her at all. Oh, no. Instead of leaving them at home to catch cold, she took them right along with her.

"Kill-deer, kill-deer," he piped as loudly as he could; "kill-deer, kill-deer."

You see, Virginia had a warm sac on her stomach. As soon as her babies were born, she put them in the sac and carried them everywhere she went. They did not come out of the sac until they were more than two months old. Even after they left the sac they did not leave their mother for another month, but clung to her long fur. Sometimes they wrapped their tails around her tail, which she held over her back, and that helped them to hang on.

There are other Feathered Friends and Furry Friends that have sacs in which they carry things also. Bigmouth the Pelican has a large pouch under his chin in which he can carry many, many fish. Satchelface the Pocket Gopher has a pocket on each side of his mouth in which he carries food and other things. Then, there is Mrs. Kangaroo of Australia, who also has a sac on her stomach in which she carries her baby.

Virginia Opossum did not walk fast. She was never in a hurry, no matter what she did. Sometimes she stopped and climbed bushes to see if she could find berries on them. At other places she stopped to dig in the ground after roots, or tried to catch a large, fat grasshopper. If she could have found the nest of Crooner the Dove, she probably would have eaten the eggs or the Baby Doves, whichever happened to be there.

Virginia thought she might find the nests of Mrs. Mallard or Mrs. Spoonbill or Mrs. Curlew or Mrs. Snipe in the Marshy Banks along the Duck Pond. Then she would have a feast if they were not watching.

Virginia walked so slowly that it was rather late when she arrived at the Marshy Banks. She was walking quietly through the Fuzzy Cattails and Tumbled Bulrushes, trying not to awaken anyone, when all at once she almost ran over Kill-deer the Plover.

"Kill-deer, kill-deer," he piped as loudly as he could; "kill-deer, kill-deer."

Of course that awakened all the little Wild Creatures, and they were on the lookout for an enemy. There was Killdeer the Plover circling around over Virginia and saying, "Kill-deer, kill-deer," everywhere she went.

So Virginia Opossum turned and started back to her Warm Hollow Log, carrying her babies with her, and feeling as a boy does when he is caught in mischief.

It was almost daylight when Virginia arrived at the Woodlot, and she was very tired. She wanted to curl up and sleep; but Virginia knew that she would have to keep going if she reached her home before the Laughing Yellow Sun came up, and the Laughing Yellow Sun told many secrets.

CHAPTER 12

Bigmouth the Pelican Goes Seining

BIGMOUTH the Pelican was fishing. He was catching a breakfast for his two babies. This is how he was doing it: He would swim across the Duck Pond, barely skimming over the water. Then suddenly he would plunge headfirst into the water with his large mouth wide open. In a few seconds he would come to the top of the water, and almost always he would be holding a fish in the big pocket under his chin.

Bigmouth always dipped up a mouthful of water, but that did not bother him. He simply waited until the water ran out the corners of his mouth, and then he swallowed the fish.

Bigmouth was a queer-looking bird. He had a

Bigmouth the Pelican was fishing, catching a breakfast for his two babies.

long beak, and under it he carried his big sac. He used his sac for seining, or rather as a dip net. It would easily hold a gallon of water.

Usually Bigmouth did not fish alone. As a rule, he lived in a colony with many of his friends, and they fished together. If they were fishing on a small lake, they would spread out in a long line and fly across it, each one beating the water with his wings to scare the fish ahead of them. Then when they had almost reached the other side, down they would go with their mouths open, and dip up as many fish as they could.

When they were through fishing they would fly back to their nests, and then what a feast the Baby Pelicans would have! Instead of being a seine, the big pocket under Bigmouth's chin was then a family dish out of which all the Baby Pelicans ate. Sometimes they would stick their bills so far down Bigmouth's throat that their heads would be entirely out of sight. How the Baby Pelicans enjoyed their fish dinner!

But this summer Bigmouth and Mrs. Pelican had decided to live at the Old Homestead. They had built a crude nest of sticks and grass in a Secret Place near Little River. It kept Bigmouth busy feeding his two babies, especially when he had to fish alone. Mrs. Pelican usually helped Big-

Baldy the Eagle swooped
down and caught the fish in
the air before it had
fallen far.

mouth feed the babies; besides, it was easier to
catch fish when they were together.

Bigmouth was not the only one who had babies
to feed. There was Osprey the Fish Hawk, who
had a nest on the side of High Cliff not far from
Aquila the Golden Eagle. Osprey had lived there
five years, and each year he had added to his nest
until it was several feet high. Osprey also had two
baby birds to feed, and that is how he happened to
be at the Duck Pond at the same time that Bigmouth the Pelican was seining.

"What a queer way to catch fish!" said Osprey
to Bigmouth, as they met at the edge of the Duck
Pond. Bigmouth was standing in the water and
draining the water from his sac after he came up
from a dive. Osprey was sitting on the limb of a
tree near by.

(76)

"It's a good way," replied Bigmouth, as he swallowed a fish.

"I like my way better," said Osprey.

Now, although Osprey undoubtedly caught larger fish than Bigmouth caught, yet Bigmouth preferred small ones, and more of them. It was a matter of personal taste. Osprey was like some folks. They think no way is quite so good as their way of doing a thing. Osprey thought he was quite the best fisherman on the Old Homestead, but there were others who were as expert in their own way and who didn't seem to care whether others thought so or not.

Longlegs the Heron preferred to stalk quietly alongshore, or stand on one foot for an hour if necessary, and spear the fish when they came within reach. Lutra the Otter dived right in after them. Then there was Alcyon the Kingfisher. Alcyon fished very much like Osprey the Fish Hawk, except that usually he sat on a high limb until he saw a fish swim beneath him and then plunged in after it. Alcyon's fish were smaller than Osprey's because Alcyon was a much smaller bird.

"I'll show you how I catch fish," said Osprey, and away he flew.

When Osprey had risen high in the air, he stayed

in one spot for a time by beating the air with his wings. His sharp eyes watched the water beneath him. Suddenly he folded his wings and shot feet first with the speed of an arrow into the water. When he came up, he was holding a fish that weighed fully a third as much as he did.

Osprey squealed with delight as he flew over Bigmouth and started toward his nest with the fish. It was the largest he had ever caught in the Duck Pond.

Now, Baldy the Eagle was very fond of fish, but he was not much of a fisherman. So he would wait until he saw Osprey flying toward his nest with a fish; then he would fly after him and take it away from him. Osprey had lost many fish that way, and he should have been more careful. He was so interested in showing Bigmouth how to catch fish that he forgot all about watching for Baldy, who was now flying toward him.

The first that Osprey knew Baldy was near was when he heard a terrible scream. Then it was too late to escape with his heavy fish. He could not fly fast enough. There was nothing for Osprey to do but to drop his fish. That was what Baldy wanted, and he swooped down and caught it in the air before it had fallen far.

Then Osprey had to go back and catch another

and carry it to his nest when Baldy the Eagle was not watching.

Baldy was like some people who do not like to work. They would rather get someone else to do their work for them; then, after it is done, they expect to enjoy the results. Baldy was worse, because he was a pirate and a bully. He could have caught his own fish, but he would rather take them from Osprey.

CHAPTER 13

Jim Crow Gets Caught

AMONG all the birds that lived on the Old Homestead, Jim Crow was about the worst. There was Pesty the Magpie, who killed Baby Bunnies, and picked Old Bent Horn until she had a sore on her side, and did many other things; and there was Tattler the Jay, who robbed the nests of other birds and bullied birds smaller than himself.

It was no wonder that Pesty the Magpie and Tattler the Jay were so mean, because they were both cousins of Jim Crow. But Jim Crow was the worst of the three.

Jim Crow really lived by plundering. He would steal the eggs and Baby Birds from the nests he found, kill Baby Bunnies, pull up Farmer Smith's corn when it was small, eat large quantities of it after it was ripe, take Fluffy Ducklets from the Duck Pond if he had a chance, rob the nests of Hungarian the Partridge and Bobby White, and even take eggs from Old Cluck the Hen if he could do it without getting caught. He was as black inside as he looked outside.

There was one thing that Jim Crow liked especially well to do. That was to pester Great Horn the Owl and Screecher the Owl and all the other owls he could find. He had a special pick at owls, and whenever he found one asleep in a tree he would call all his friends together to tease it.

"Caw-caw-caw," he would call, as loud as he could; "I have found Screecher asleep. Come over and help me to tease him."

Then Jim Crow and his friends would gather around on the tree near Screecher the Owl, cawing and scolding and threatening. There was simply no use for Screecher to try to sleep when they were around, and there was no chance to fly away and hide. They would all follow with loud caws and make an awful noise. Screecher needed sleep so much after being up all night.

It would seem that Screecher could defend himself with his needlelike claws and sharp beak, but perhaps he cannot see well enough in the bright light. You see, Screecher's eyes are made so he can see at night, and the bright daylight hurts them. Hunting Cat can also see well in the dark, but he does not mind daylight. His eyes adjust themselves to the light.

Fearful the Man knew that Jim Crow and his friends liked to tease Screecher the Owl. So once upon a time he decided he would get even with

Jim Crow and his family for all the mean deeds they had done. Fearful the Man had a scheme which he thought would work if he were careful.

Jim Crow and his friends were shrewd. They were careful not to let Fearful the Man get close enough to them to shoot them. But Fearful thought he had a plan that would fool Jim Crow, and so he had.

First he gathered a basketful of gray and white feathers from the yard. Then he made a cloth owl and covered it with the feathers. It looked like Screecher the Owl when it was finished. Its wings were loose so they would move when Fearful the Man pulled a string.

When all was ready, Fearful the Man took his gun and the cloth owl and went to a field. He fastened the cloth owl in a tree, and then hid with

Scrapper the Kingbird was not afraid of Jim Crow, even though he was not half so large.

There was simply no use for Screecher to try to sleep when Jim Crow and his friends were around.

his gun in a patch of weeds near the tree. He had a long string running from the cloth owl to his Hiding Place, and when he was hidden he pulled the string and the cloth owl seemed to move its wings.

It was not long until the sharp eyes of Jim Crow spied the cloth owl. He thought surely it was Screecher the Owl.

"Caw-caw-caw, caw-caw-caw," he yelled to his friends, "I spy Screecher the Owl. Let's fly over and tease him awhile."

Soon Jim Crow and all his friends were in the tree by the cloth owl, cawing and scolding and threatening. They were so interested in pestering the cloth owl that they did not stop to look for Fearful the Man. They had no idea that he was near until they heard a loud explosion.

"Boom, boom," went Fearful's gun, and down fell two of Jim Crow's friends.

But even that did not teach Jim Crow a lesson. He is a born criminal and is always looking for some mischief to get into.

One day he spied the nest of Yellowbreast the Chat. It was not strange that he saw it, for Yellowbreast had built it in a low bush and had made no attempt to hide it. In fact, it was in plain sight. Yellowbreast the Chat belonged to the big family of Warblers, which included Pinky the Redstart and Chirper the Ovenbird.

When Jim Crow found Yellowbreast's nest with five Baby Chats in it, he hopped right down by it and was all ready to make a meal of the Baby Chats. Jim Crow knew that Yellowbreast was not much of a fighter, and he was not afraid of Yellowbreast.

But there was one bird watching that Jim Crow had not seen. That was Scrapper the Kingbird. He was sitting on his Lookout Stub guarding the nests of all his Feathered Friends around there. Scrapper was one bird that was not afraid of Jim Crow even though he was not half so large; and Jim Crow knew it. He also knew that Scrapper did not like him, for he could remember the sharp jabs of Scrapper's bill that he had felt several times.

So he always tried to stay away from Scrapper.

Scrapper saw that Jim Crow had found Yellow-breast's nest, and he knew that the Baby Chats would not last long unless something were done. The first thing Jim Crow knew, Scrapper was right on top of him and was making his black feathers fly. That was the last time Jim came to that part of the Old Homestead in a good long time.

Whenever the Feathered Friends saw Scrapper the Kingbird on his Lookout Stub, they knew they were safe from Jim Crow and Sharpshin the Hawk and other enemies, for Scrapper was a good police-man of the air.

CHAPTER 14

The Muskrats Have a Visitor

JIMMY the Swamp Rabbit lived in the Tumbled Bulrushes and Jungle Thickets by the Duck Pond. He was a first cousin of Molly Cottontail and Peter, who lived in a Friendly Burrow in the Little Jungle Thicket at the foot of High Cliff. Sometimes Molly came down to the Duck Pond for a visit with Jimmy. She liked to run through the Tumbled Bulrushes and Jungle Thickets almost as well as Jimmy did.

Jimmy did not live in a Friendly Burrow such as Molly lived in. He had built a Covered Nest out of Swamp Grass and Dancing Little Leaflets, and had lined it with some of his own fur. It was right in the middle of a large clump of Fuzzy Cattails, and it had a doorway on one side.

When Jimmy first built his home, the clump of Fuzzy Cattails was completely surrounded with water. Jimmy thought that would be a good protection from Snoop the Weasel, Reddy Fox, and other of his enemies who did not like water.

You see, Jimmy the Swamp Rabbit was not like Molly and Peter when it came to water. They would not have thought of going into water unless

Jimmy the Swamp
Rabbit lived in the Tumbled Bulrushes and Jungle Thickets
by the Duck Pond.

they were forced to do so. But Jimmy liked to
swim as much as did Trailer the Mink. So he had
built his Covered Nest where it was entirely surrounded with water, for he did not mind swimming when he left it to go into the Jungle Thickets.
It really was quite a protection from Snoop the
Weasel.

Some time after Jimmy built his Covered Nest,
the water in the Duck Pond began to get lower.
It always was lower during the summer. After a
while Jimmy's Covered Nest did not have any
water around it at all. Then Snoop the Weasel had
no trouble tracking Jimmy right to his home.

Always when Snoop was tracking Jimmy and
Jimmy's trail came to the edge of the water, Snoop
could go no farther, because the Playful Air Whiffs

did not tell Snoop which way Jimmy had gone. Then Snoop would have to go hunting some other place.

Snoop the Weasel was a cousin of Lutra the Otter, Trailer the Mink, Killer the Marten, and Fisher the Bold. He was also related to Mephitis the Skunk, Carcajou the Glutton, and Digger the Badger. Snoop was the smallest of his family, but he was ferocious. That is, he was bloodthirsty. He would kill much more than he could ever eat.

Once Snoop the Weasel got into Farmer Smith's henhouse. It was not because he was hungry, for he had plenty to eat. All he wanted to do was to kill some chickens for the fun of it. He did not eat any of them, but he did drink some of the blood. If Farmer Smith could have found Snoop right then, it would have been the last of Snoop.

Yes, sir, Snoop was an out-and-out villain, and Jimmy the Swamp Rabbit had good reason to be afraid of him. But there was one who could make Snoop the Weasel hunt a hole, and that was Reddy Fox. Whenever Reddy Fox came along, Snoop knew it was time to hide.

One day Snoop was out hunting as usual. He liked to hunt during the day as well as at night, and he liked to hunt in the winter as well as in the summer. During the winter Snoop wore a white coat, and in summer he wore a brown one. That was so he could sneak through the snow in winter or through grass and brush in summer and not be easily seen.

On this day he wore his brown coat, and it would have taken a sharp eye to see him as he trailed through the brush and grass and over rocks. He had been looking for Tiny the Meadow Mouse and Tawny Chipmunk and Miner the Mole.

Then he crossed through the Green Meadow, hoping that he would find Ringneck the Pheasant and his family or Burlingame the Meadow Lark. After that he started for the Duck Pond. You see, Snoop the Weasel was quite a traveler, and he thought he might catch one of the Mallards or Spoonbills or Jimmy the Swamp Rabbit at the Duck Pond.

Snoop the Weasel was an out-and-out villain.

Almost the first thing, Snoop found the trail of Jimmy. Jimmy had been eating some of the Tender Grass Shoots that grew in the Jungle Thicket by the Duck Pond. When he was no longer hungry, he had gone to his Covered Nest for a rest.

Snoop the Weasel had no trouble following Jimmy's trail. Snoop's nose was as keen-scented as Nero the Hound's. He trailed Jimmy here and there through the Swamp Grass and right down to where the edge of the Duck Pond had been. That was where Snoop had always lost Jimmy's trail before. But this time there was no water, and Snoop went along sniffing until he came right to Jimmy's Covered Nest.

Jimmy was not so foolish as he might have been. Instead of going to sleep, he sat there with his eyes looking out his doorway watching his trail. Before Snoop could get close enough to grab him, Jimmy bounded out of his Covered Nest and down to the Duck Pond. Then he jumped into the water and started to swim as fast as he could.

Out among the Fuzzy Cattails Jimmy could see the Grassy House of Danny Muskrat. In a little while he reached it and climbed up on top, quite out of breath, but so very happy that he was still alive.

"Oh, such a narrow escape!" gasped Jimmy.

"Why are you so out of breath?" asked Danny Muskrat.

Jimmy told him the whole story of how he had disappointed Snoop the Weasel, who could not swim so fast as he could.

"Why do you not build your Covered Nest away out in the water?" asked Danny Muskrat.

"I did," answered Jimmy, "but the water went down, and soon it was all dry ground around my house. But I am going to build myself a new Covered Nest where I am sure the water will stay around it."

So Jimmy the Swamp Rabbit started out to find a clump of Tumbled Bulrushes that was entirely surrounded with water, where he could make another Covered Nest.

CHAPTER 15

Danny Muskrat Finds Something Good

THE Grassy House of Danny Muskrat was one place where few enemies came. It was built of Tumbled Bulrushes, Fuzzy Cattails, Oozy Mud, and Swamp Grass. One reason why it was quite safe was that it was too far from land for most enemies like Reddy Fox and Ranger the Coyote to venture. But the main reason was that Danny's doorway was completely under water, and no one knew where it was but himself and Mrs. Muskrat.

When Danny built his Grassy House, he first made a big pile of Tumbled Bulrushes and Oozy Mud that rested on the bottom of the Duck Pond and with the top, which was to be his floor, above water. He left a hole in the middle of this pile, and under the pile he dug a trench for a doorway that led to the hole in the center. Then he could dive to the trench, follow through it to the hole in the middle, and come right up into his home. He carried more Tumbled Bulrushes and Swamp Grass and Oozy Mud and Moss and built a large round house on top of the pile. In it was a bedroom.

No one dared to venture into Danny Muskrat's home, for he was a fierce fighter when necessary.

When Danny was tired of swimming around in the Duck Pond and digging up Juicy Water Bulbs to eat, he could go home and sleep.

No, there was no one who dared to venture into Danny Muskrat's home. Danny had long, sharp teeth, and he was a fierce fighter when he had to be. If Danny was let alone, he was peaceful, except that he found Fluffy Ducklets a temptation sometimes if they came too near.

Danny's favorite food was Juicy Water Bulbs and Sweet Cattail Stalks that grew all around his home. Whenever he wanted something to eat, down he would dive, and in a minute or two he would come up with his dinner. Sometimes he sat on top of his house while he ate it, and sometimes he went inside. If Danny Muskrat wanted to, he

(93)

could stay under water a long, long time while he was digging.

One day Danny went for a swim around the Duck Pond. In and out among the Sheltered Water Lanes that ran through the Fuzzy Cattails he swam. At last he became hungry, and he began to look for a Sweet Cattail Stalk to cut down and eat.

"I believe this one will be good," he said to himself, as he took a nibble to see how it tasted.

"Oh, pl-*ease;* oh, pl-*ease,*" sang some one overhead.

Danny Muskrat looked up to see who was there, and saw Redwing the Blackbird sitting on a Fuzzy Cattail.

"Oh, pl-*ease* do not cut down that Sweet Cattail Stalk," said Redwing; "it is holding up my nest."

Danny Muskrat and Redwing were good friends. Danny liked to hear Redwing sing. Sometimes when enemies came near, Redwing stopped singing and said "Chack-chack." Then Danny knew it was time to dive out of sight.

"I did not know that that was your Sweet Cattail Stalk," said Danny. "I am sure I do not need it, for there are many more."

"O-thank-you," said Redwing.

So Danny went to look for a Juicy Water Bulb,

while Redwing the Blackbird sang happily: "Oak-a-*lee,* oak-a-*lee.*"

Danny Muskrat did not always stay in the water. Sometimes he went exploring in the Fresh Earth Fields near the Duck Pond. In fact, he had sometimes gone over to Little River to visit some friends. Danny's friends that lived along Little River did not live in a Grassy House. They lived in a Hidden Den in the bank. Their doorway was deep under water, like the doorway to Danny's Grassy House. Anyone passing by would never have dreamed there was a Hidden Den in the bank.

It was strange that Danny liked to live at the Duck Pond in a Grassy House while his friends preferred to live in a Hidden Den in the bank of Little River. Perhaps it was for the same reason that some people live in the city and others in the country; and some live in brick houses, while others own wood ones. Then again, some folks like one state, while others want a different one.

Danny Muskrat was like most people; he liked to go visiting. So one evening, as the Smiling Moon was peeping over the Black Tree Tops, Danny thought it would be a good time to go to visit his friends on Little River.

Danny dived off his Grassy House and swam toward shore. He made little Golden Ripples on

the water wherever the Smiling Moon touched
them. When he reached the shore, he climbed up
the muddy bank and started right through the
Jungle Thicket that was between him and the
Fresh Earth Field that he was to cross on his way
to Little River.

It was a foolish thing for Danny Muskrat to do,
leaving the water that way. He did not know what
minute Great Horn the Owl might swoop down
upon him, or Ranger the Coyote come running
across the field.

When Danny reached the edge of the Jungle
Thicket, he stopped and looked across the Fresh
Earth Field. Everything looked safe enough, and
he started across. Danny had not gone far when
he smelled something good. It did not smell like
the Juicy Water Bulbs or the Sweet Cattail Stalks
that he found in the Duck Pond. But it was something good to eat; Danny was sure of that.

Danny dug down into the Soft Warm Ground.
It was no time at all until he had pulled out one
of the Sweet Smelling Rootlets, and had taken a
nibble off one end.

"Yum, yum," said Danny Muskrat; "Golden
Yellow Carrots!"

Danny ate that Golden Yellow Carrot and another. Then he dug up a fine large one and started

back with it for Mrs. Muskrat. He forgot entirely about going over to Little River to visit his friends.

The next day Bud and Mary Smith were walking across the Fresh Earth Field. Bud noticed where Danny Muskrat had dug up the Golden Yellow Carrots.

"Oh, see here," said Bud, "Danny Muskrat has found the Golden Yellow Carrots I planted for him. I am so glad."

CHAPTER 16

The Fluffy Ducklets Appear

ALL the little Wild Creatures on the Old Homestead were wondering what had become of Mrs. Mallard. No one had seen her for a long time. You see, when Mrs. Mallard was sitting on her eggs in her nest, and she wanted a drink, she was careful to sneak down to the Duck Pond and back to her Nesting Place when no one could see her. She was afraid someone might steal her eggs. So all the little Wild Creatures were wondering what had happened to her.

"I wonder what has become of Mrs. Mallard," said Redwing the Blackbird to Jimmy the Swamp Rabbit when they met one day; "I haven't seen her for a long, long time."

"Perhaps Snoop the Weasel caught her," said Jimmy the Swamp Rabbit; "he tried to catch me, and almost scared me to death."

"I wonder what has happened to Mrs. Mallard," said Longlegs the Heron to Diver the Grebe.

"Perhaps Terror the Hunter shot her," said Diver the Grebe; "he tried to shoot me."

"I wonder where Mrs. Mallard is," said Jack Snipe to Midget the Teal.

"Perhaps Trailer the Mink caught her," said Midget the Teal; "he almost got me."

"Where do you suppose Mrs. Mallard has gone?" asked Boomer the Bittern of Great Diver the Loon. "It has been a long time since I have seen her."

"Perhaps Sharptoes the Duck Hawk killed her," said Great Diver; "he tried to get Mr. Mallard when he was visiting with me."

All the little Wild Creatures were wondering.

"I believe I'll ask Mr. Mallard when I see him," said Redwing the Blackbird to Jimmy the Swamp Rabbit.

"I shall find Mr. Mallard and ask him," said Longlegs the Heron to Diver the Grebe.

Have you asked Mr. Mallard?" said Midget the Teal to Jack Snipe.

"Suppose we see what Mr. Mallard says," suggested Great Diver the Loon to Boomer the Bittern. So away they all went to find Mr. Mallard.

But Mr. Mallard only went about his business of hunting something to eat, and said nothing.

Bud and Mary Smith were also wondering about Mrs. Mallard, but neither said anything to the other.

"I wonder when Mrs. Mallard's eggs will hatch," is what Bud was thinking to himself. "I believe I'll sneak down to the Duck Pond and see if there are any Fluffy Ducklets in sight yet. Won't that be fun to tell Mary about them?" And away went Bud toward the Duck Pond when Mary was not watching.

"I wonder if Mrs. Mallard really is on her nest all this time," said Mary to herself. "I am afraid that something has happened to her. I think I will run down to the Duck Pond while Bud is not here, and see if there are any Fluffy Ducklets. It would be so much fun to see them first and then tell Bud." Away slipped Mary through the Apple Orchard so she would be sure Bud would not see her.

Bud ran swiftly until he came to the Jungle Thicket along the Duck Pond. Then he began to crawl slowly through the bushes and vines and

There were Mr. and Mrs. Mallard and
ten Fluffy Ducklets out for a swim.

tall grass toward an open place where he could look out across the water.

In a short time Bud thought he heard a noise in the Jungle Thicket, and he stopped to listen. Sure enough, something was snapping twigs and rubbing against the brush. It sounded as if the noise was coming his way. Bud stretched out on the ground out of sight in the Jungle Thicket. Nearer and nearer came the noise.

At last Bud sat up carefully and looked through a large bush that was in front of him, and what do you suppose he saw in the Jungle Thicket ahead of him? Why, Mary's red hat.

"Now, isn't that just like a girl?" thought Bud. "Trying to sneak through the Jungle Thicket, with a hat on one could see a mile." But Mary's sharp eyes had spied Bud's sweaty face shining through the bush, and it was useless for him to try to hide longer.

"What are you doing here?" asked Bud, as Mary came up.

"What are *you* doing here?" said Mary.

"Oh, I just thought I'd come over to see—well —I was wondering about Mrs. Mallard," replied Bud.

"Thought you would be the first to see the Fluffy Ducklets, if there were any, didn't you?"

said Mary. "But you're not, because I am going right along."

"Well, I suppose it is all right," said Bud; "but if you are going with me, you will have to take off that red hat. A fine scout you'd be!"

Mary removed her hat and crept along behind Bud. The sticks hurt her knees sometimes, but she did not mind that. She was a little worried, though, when one caught in her stocking and tore a big hole in it.

"Now, just see what I've done!" said Mary.

"Psst, not so loud," whispered Bud. "Let's take a peep and see if there is anything in sight."

Bud and Mary rose up slowly and looked through the Fuzzy Cattails and Tumbled Bulrushes.

"Oh!" they both exclaimed at once, for right there in front of them, and not half as far as Bud could have thrown a stone, were Mr. and Mrs. Mallard and ten Fluffy Ducklets. Mr. Mallard was swimming around as proud of his family as anything, and Mrs. Mallard was having a time to keep her babies together on their first swim.

"Let's run home and tell Dad and Mother," said Mary.

CHAPTER 17

Billy Coon Makes Some Plans

BILLY COON lived in a Hollow Den Tree near the end of the bridge that crossed Little River. He lived a rather peaceful life, for he had few enemies. Of course, if Nero the Hound or Ranger the Coyote or Shaggy the Wolf got on his trail, his life was not so peaceful for a while. But Billy Coon usually stayed near trees, and if an enemy came near, up a tree he would go; and there he would stay until the enemy left. Nero the Hound and Ranger the Coyote and Shaggy the Wolf could not climb a tree, so Billy Coon was quite safe.

Billy Coon had a special reason for living near Little River. He could have found any number of Hollow Den Trees in the Black Forest. He liked to swim; but the main reason why Billy Coon lived near Little River was that he liked to catch small fish and hunt Pinkshell the Clam and Pinchtoe the Crawfish. He also liked to eat corn sometimes that grew in the Fresh Earth Field not far away. He did not care whether it was green or ripe. Most of the Furry Friends ate either all meat as Lutra the Otter did, or all vegetable food as Danny Muskrat did; but Billy Coon ate both. Of course, Danny Muskrat sometimes ate clams and such things, but he really preferred Juicy Water Bulbs.

Another reason why Billy Coon liked to live near Little River was that he preferred to wash his food before he ate it. If he found something good to eat, he took it in his front feet, which he used like hands, and soused it in the water. Billy Coon was clean about his eating.

Billy Coon was like some people in one way, he was curious. If he saw something shining in the water, he had to find out what it was. He would pounce upon it with his front feet and then take it up to examine it. Perhaps he thought that most bright objects in the water were clams or fish, and he jumped on them to catch them; but that habit was once almost the death of Billy Coon.

You see, it happened like this: Trapper Jim knew that Billy Coon was curious. He knew that if Billy Coon saw something shining in the water, he would jump on it. So Trapper Jim fastened a Shiny Tin Fish on the pan of a trap, and set the trap under water where Billy Coon would see it. He thought Billy Coon would pounce on the Shiny Tin Fish and be caught.

Sure enough, when Billy Coon came along that night, he jumped with both front feet on the Shiny

Billy Coon lived in his Hollow Den Tree near the end of the bridge that crossed Little River.

Tin Fish. Snap went the trap, and Billy Coon would have been a prisoner if a Round Pebble had not held the jaws of the trap apart. But even that did not make Billy Coon stop poking his feet into holes to see what he could find.

One evening about dusk Billy Coon started out on his regular nightly stroll. He had been sleeping all day in his Hollow Den Tree and felt hungry. He thought a Creamy Roasting Ear would taste good, so, when he came down from his Hollow Den Tree, he started toward the Rustling Cornfield over near the Duck Pond.

Billy Coon liked to ramble through the Jungle Thicket and Tumbled Bulrushes along the Duck Pond sometimes. He would hunt for wild berries awhile in the Jungle Thicket, and then he would

(105)

look for Croaker the Frog, Pinchtoe the Crawfish, and Pinkshell the Clam along the banks of the Duck Pond. He thought it was great fun wading along in the Oozy Mud.

Billy Coon made a queer track. Bud Smith could always tell Billy's track from Virginia Opossum's and others'. It looked almost as if a barefooted baby had walked along. That was because Billy used part of his leg as well as his foot to walk on behind. Growler the Bear also walked like that.

After Billy Coon had eaten his fill of green corn, he started for the Duck Pond. It had been quite a while since he had visited the Duck Pond, and he thought he would find something good to finish his meal. The Smiling Moon was shining, and Croaker the Frog was making a loud noise among the Lily Pads.

"Have you heard the news?" asked Digger the Badger, as he made the dirt fly.

"I shall have no trouble finding Croaker," thought Billy Coon, "and then I will pounce on him before he sees me."

At the edge of the Rustling Cornfield Billy Coon saw Digger the Badger. Digger was busy trying to dig out Satchelface the Pocket Gopher, but Satchelface always managed to find a Secret Little Tunnel through which to escape. Satchelface had a pocket on each side of his face in which he put corn and grass and other food that he wanted to carry to his Secret Storehouse. Then he could eat it whenever he was hungry. Sometimes he carried dirt out of his Friendly Burrow in his pockets when he was making a new Secret Tunnel.

"Have you heard the news?" asked Digger the Badger, as he made the dirt fly.

"No, what is it?" said Billy Coon.

"Mephitis the Skunk told me that Jimmy the Swamp Rabbit told him that the Mallards have ten Fluffy Ducklets, and he thinks Trailer the Mink is waiting for a chance to catch them and make a meal of them."

When Billy Coon heard that, he did not wait to visit any more. No, sir. He hopped out of the Rustling Cornfield and right into the Jungle Thicket. He did not even stop to see if he could find some Tempting Berries.

"I think I shall try to catch those Fluffy Ducklets myself," he said, as he left the Jungle Thicket and started into the Tumbled Bulrushes along the Duck Pond. "I wonder where those Fluffy Ducklets are."

Of course Digger the Badger was too busy looking for Satchelface the Gopher to notice where Billy Coon went. He was trying to find which Secret Little Tunnel Satchelface was hiding in.

CHAPTER 18

The Ducklets Take a Swim

THE Fluffy Ducklets were already five days old when Billy Coon heard about them. They had swum around their Sheltered Little Cove many times with Mr. and Mrs. Mallard, and were beginning to feel quite grown up. They could find their own Wriggly Waterworms and Wild Rice and could stand on their heads in the water almost as well as could Mrs. Mallard.

Of course, the Fluffy Ducklets could not reach the Oozy Mud in the bottom of the Duck Pond in as deep water as their mother could. Their necks were not long enough. So they had to stay near shore when they were playing the game of Tip-up. They liked to play Tip-up with Mother Mallard, because sometimes she reached away down in the water and pulled up a large bunch of Green Water Moss for them to pick at.

One night when the Fluffy Ducklets were playing around in the Sheltered Little Cove, Ducky Waddles spied a Sheltered Water Lane. He had not noticed it before, and it looked interesting.

"Oh, Mother, where does that Sheltered Water Lane go?" he asked.

(109)

"You come right back here," quacked Mother Mallard.

"But, Mother, I want to see what is at the end of the Sheltered Water Lane." So Mrs. Mallard decided she would take the Fluffy Ducklets out to see the Duck Pond.

Down the Sheltered Water Lane swam Mrs. Mallard, with all the Fluffy Ducklets following behind. First there was Ducky Waddles and then Ducky Doodles, and behind them were Ducky Diver and the other Fluffy Ducklets.

"Now, Ducklets, don't get lost," said Mrs. Mallard as they neared the end of the Sheltered Water Lane. It was the first long swim the Fluffy Ducklets had taken, and Mrs. Mallard was afraid they could not find their way back to the Sheltered Little Cove without her.

The Fluffy Ducklets liked to play Tip-up with Mother Mallard, because sometimes she pulled up a large bunch of Green Water Moss for them.

"No, no," said the Fluffy Ducklets; "we will stay near you, Mother."

At last they came to the end of the Sheltered Water Lane and looked out. The Duck Pond looked almost as large as an ocean to the Fluffy Ducklets.

"Oh, oh!" they all exclaimed, as they tried to flap their tiny wings. "Let's swim around it."

"Not tonight," said Mrs. Mallard; "the Smiling Moon is shining brightly, and Great Horn the Owl or Sharptoes the Duck Hawk might get you. You must stay out of sight among the Fuzzy Cattails."

Ducky Doodles thought he was quite grown-up. He thought he would swim a little way by himself, and see what he could find among the Fuzzy Cattails. He was like some boys and girls who think they know better than their parents what is good for them.

So while the other Fluffy Ducklets played Tip-up near the Sheltered Water Lane, Ducky Doodles started along the edge of the Duck Pond when Mr. and Mrs. Mallard did not see him. And away he swam!

About this time Billy Coon arrived at the Duck Pond. "I wonder where those Fluffy Ducklets are," thought Billy Coon. "I believe I will start around the Duck Pond and find their Landing Place."

You see, Billy Coon knew that the Fluffy Ducklets could not stay on the water all the time. He knew that sometimes they would have to come to shore for a rest and sleep. Of course, after they were a little larger, they could tuck their bills under their wings and sleep right on the water. But they did not yet have wings, so they cuddled near their mother to keep warm while they slept.

Billy Coon knew that as soon as they were tired out they would come back to the bank. He thought if he could find their Landing Place, he would wait until they came back to shore and then pounce on them. So he started walking slowly around the Duck Pond.

Billy Coon was not in a hurry. He was hunting for good things to eat along the Marshy Banks as he walked along. But then, he was never in a hurry except when Nero the Hound was after him. He was not afraid as long as he was near the Duck Pond. If an enemy came by, he would run into the water. Then if he had to, he could fight. Billy Coon could fight much better in water than on land.

There was not much chance of meeting Nero the Hound after dark, for Nero stayed by the Ram-

Down the Sheltered Water Lane swam Mrs. Mallard,
with all the Fluffy Ducklets following behind.

bling Old Barn at night to keep away prowlers.
Shaggy the Wolf was probably in the Black Forest
looking for Snowshoe the Hare, and Ranger the
Coyote was no doubt hunting Snowshoe's big
cousin Jack the Jumper in the Wide-Wide Pasture.

So Billy Coon felt quite safe. He really played
along the Marshy Bank longer than he should
have done, for it was getting daylight before he
was halfway around. It was almost time for the
Laughing Yellow Sun to peep over the eastern
hills as the Smiling Moon was nodding behind the
treetops in the Black Forest.

"I believe I'd better find a Hiding Place and go
to sleep," said Billy Coon to himself; "then I can
finish looking for the Fluffy Ducklets tomorrow
night."

It did not take him long to find a Hiding Place. He had explored the Old Homestead so much he knew where everyone was located. In the Wood Lot, not far from the home of Virginia Opossum, he found a Warm Hollow Log. No one was living in it, except that sometimes Jimmy the Swamp Rabbit ran into it to hide.

In a little while Billy Coon was sound asleep and dreaming about chasing Fluffy Ducklets through Tumbled Bulrushes at the Duck Pond.

No doubt Trailer the Mink was dreaming about the same thing in his Hidden Den near the bank of Little River. Do you suppose either of their dreams really happened?

CHAPTER 19

Alcyon the Kingfisher Proves a Friend

"NOW where do you suppose Ducky Doodles is?" said Mrs. Mallard, as the rest of the Fluffy Ducklets climbed up the Marshy Bank in the Sheltered Little Cove. It was about the same time that Billy Coon was crawling into the Warm Hollow Log to go to sleep.

"I suppose he got lost in the Fuzzy Cattails along the Sheltered Water Lane," said Mr. Mallard. "I'll look for him."

"You stay right here and watch these Fluffy Ducklets, and I will go and look for him," said Mrs. Mallard. "I can quack louder than you can. I'm going right this minute."

So away hurried Mrs. Mallard to hunt for Ducky Doodles, while Mr. Mallard led the Fluffy Ducklets to a Hiding Place among the Tumbled Bulrushes.

"Qua-ack quack-quack-quack," called Mrs. Mallard loudly, as she swam down the Sheltered Water Lane. "Qua-ack quack-quack-quack."

The Mallards always took the Fluffy Ducklets for a swim at night because they thought it would be safer on the water than on land. They knew

(115)

As the Fluffy Ducklets were ready to walk up the Marshy Bank, there was a loud noise overhead. It was Alcyon the Kingfisher.

that Trailer the Mink and Billy Coon and Snoop the Weasel and other Night Prowlers might get them if they stayed on land at night. But they did not fear them during the day. If they were in sight on the water during the day, they knew that Sharptoes the Duck Hawk might see them.

Of course, if the Fluffy Ducklets wanted to play in the water during the day, they could do so in the Sheltered Little Cove where Sharptoes could not see them. But usually the Fluffy Ducklets were ready to rest awhile after playing in the water almost all night.

Mrs. Mallard swam almost to the end of the Sheltered Water Lane. "Qua-ack quack-quack-quack," she called again, for she had expected to find Ducky Doodles not far away. Although Mrs. Mallard swam here and there, and quacked and quacked, there was no Ducky Doodles to be found. "I do hope that Danny Muskrat did not catch him," she said, as she started back to the Sheltered Little Cove.

That night as Billy Coon left the Warm Hollow Log and started around the Duck Pond to find the Fluffy Ducklets, Mr. and Mrs. Mallard and the Fluffy Ducklets started out to see if they could find Ducky Doodles.

The first thing Billy Coon did when he reached the Duck Pond was to take a bath. Then he walked along the bank in the Oozy Mud looking for a breakfast. It was a queer time to be eating breakfast, when Bud and Mary were eating supper; but it really was Billy Coon's breakfast, for he had slept all day.

After a while Billy Coon came to the Sheltered Little Cove. He could see duck feathers on the Marshy Bank, and there were many, many Ducklet Tracks in the Oozy Mud. Billy Coon sniffed around awhile and followed the Ducklet Tracks up the Marshy Bank to the place where the Fluffy Ducklets had stayed that day.

"Aha," said Billy Coon. "I have found where the Fluffy Ducklets stay at last. I'll hunt around in the Jungle Thicket for Tempting Berries for a while, and then come back after the Fluffy

Ducklets when it is time for them to come ashore."
Away strolled Billy Coon.

Now, when the Mallards and the Fluffy Ducklets reached the end of the Sheltered Water Lane,
Mrs. Mallard quacked loudly to see if she could
call Ducky Doodles. Far across the Duck Pond
there was a loud quack in answer.

"That was Mrs. Spoonbill," said Mrs. Mallard.
"Suppose we swim over and ask her if she has seen
Ducky Doodles."

Away swam the Mallards and the Fluffy Ducklets, with Mrs. Mallard quacking every now and
then to let Mrs. Spoonbill know they were coming.

In a little while they could see the Spoonbills
swimming toward them. But there were more
than just Shoveler and Mrs. Spoonbill. Yes, sir.
Close behind them were a number of Downy
Spoonbills swimming along as fast as their little
webbed feet could push them; and who else do
you suppose was right in the midst of them?
Why, Ducky Doodles, of course.

"Ducky Doodles, where have you been?"
quacked Mrs. Mallard.

"Oh, Mother, I was lost," said Ducky Doodles.
"I swam into the Tumbled Bulrushes to play with
the Downy Spoonbills, and when I came out I
could not find you."

Among the Downy
Spoonbills was
Ducky Doodles.

Ducky Doodles was glad to be with his own
brothers and sisters again, and after that he was
careful not to leave them.

It was a happy family of Mallards that started
back toward the Sheltered Water Lane that led to
the Sheltered Little Cove. They quacked and
splashed, and Billy had no trouble at all to hear
them coming.

Billy Coon was hidden in a clump of Tumbled
Bulrushes right near where the Mallards and
Fluffy Ducklets would walk up the Marshy Bank.
It was getting daylight, but Billy Coon thought he
would have time to catch some Fluffy Ducklets
and then hurry back to the Warm Hollow Log in
the Woodlot for another sleep.

Billy Coon did not know that the Mallards had

a friend near who was watching him. He thought he was well hidden in the Tumbled Bulrushes.

As the Fluffy Ducklets were ready to walk up the Marshy Bank, there was a loud noise overhead. It sounded something like a giant rattle. It was Alcyon the Kingfisher. Mr. and Mrs. Mallard called the Fluffy Ducklets back to the water. They knew that Alcyon's sharp eyes had seen danger near. Alcyon had such sharp eyes that he could see fish swimming in the water far below while he was sitting on a High Perch, and he had seen Billy Coon.

Of course, Billy Coon felt cheap, and he sneaked back to the Warm Hollow Log, knowing that the Mallards would be too smart to be caught like that again.

CHAPTER 20

Ranger the Coyote Meets His Match

RANGER the Coyote lived in a Hidden Den in the side of a hill far beyond the Wide-Wide Pasture. He liked to live there because the dry hillside grass was the color of his tawny fur, and he could hide easily. Ranger seldom went into his Hidden Den himself. He left that for Mrs. Coyote and their Furry Little Pups. Usually Ranger the Coyote stayed on a high hill where he could see if Fearful the Man came by. Then he could warn Mrs. Coyote. If Fearful the Man saw him, Ranger would run away out of range of his gun. He would sit until Fearful the Man came near, and away he would go again and sit on another knoll until Fearful came near. That was one of Ranger's tricks to lure Fearful the Man away from his Hidden Den.

Sometimes Ranger the Coyote made excursions across the Wide-Wide Pasture and through the Green Meadow and came near the Grand Old House in the hope of finding Old Cluck and her Chicklets far enough away from shelter so that he could catch them. Of course, Ranger the Coyote was always careful to make his visit in the evening or early morning, for then he was not so likely to be seen. On the way to the Old Homestead, Ranger liked to hunt for rabbits and gophers and other things to carry back to his Furry Little Pups.

One evening, when the Long Shadows were stealing out of the Black Forest and covering the Great Wide World, Ranger the Coyote left his Lookout Post near his Hidden Den and started toward the Grand Old House. You see, Old Cluck's Chicklets were getting quite large, and Mrs. Smith gave them more freedom because she thought they could take care of themselves. Ranger the Coyote had seen them hunting grasshoppers in the Green Meadow several times, but always they were too near to the Grand Old House for him to venture to catch one. Or they left and went to their roost before it was dark enough for

Ranger the Coyote started toward the Grand Old House.

him to come closer. Or else Nero the Hound was watching. No, sir; Ranger the Coyote never had been able to catch one of Old Cluck's Chicklets, but he thought that if he kept on trying, one day he would surely get one.

It happened that as Ranger the Coyote came to the Green Meadow, Ringneck the Pheasant came out of hiding for his evening meal. That was the time that Ringneck liked to catch bugs and grasshoppers, and eat Clover Leaves. Ranger the Coyote knew that it was no easy matter to catch Ringneck the Pheasant. It was not anywhere near so easy to catch Ringneck as it was Old Cluck, for Ringneck could fly away when danger came near, if he knew it.

Ranger the Coyote decided he would try to catch Ringneck, anyway. It was still a little too early for him to venture near to the Grand Old House. If he failed to get Ringneck, then he could go after one of Old Cluck's Chicklets later.

Ringneck's parents were foreigners like Hungarian the Partridge. They were brought to this country from far-off China years ago, and for that reason Ringneck was sometimes called the Chinese Pheasant. But Ringneck's family has lived here so long that the Pheasants are now quite as much at home as they were in their native land, and they are very good citizens. Ringneck was hatched on the Old Homestead, and he had learned to watch out for Ranger the Coyote and other enemies; but Ranger thought he might be caught napping. Ranger the Coyote hoped that Ringneck would be so interested in finding his supper that he would not be as watchful as usual.

Ranger ran to a good hiding place as near to Ringneck as he dared to go without being seen, and waited for him to come nearer. He also waited for it to grow darker. Ranger the Coyote is not as good as Reddy Fox when it comes to sneaking on his game. He is better at catching it in a fair chase like his big brother Shaggy the Wolf. Instead of trying to sneak nearer to Ringneck, he simply hid in the grass and waited for Ringneck to come near enough so that he could make a run for him.

Nero the Hound had been sleeping on the front lawn near the Grand Old House. That is, he had been napping with one eye open. Suddenly he thought he smelled Coyote. The Playful Air Whiffs had danced across the Green Meadow from Ranger the Coyote straight to Nero's nose. Nero sat up and looked. For a while he could see nothing, but the Playful Air Whiffs told him as plain as daylight that Ranger was not far away.

Soon Nero could see Ranger watching Ringneck the Pheasant.

Nero stood up and stretched. The hair on his back bristled. Down toward the Green Meadow he trotted with the Playful Air Whiffs bringing Coyote scent stronger and stronger as he went. Soon he was near enough to see Ranger the Coyote watching Ringneck the Pheasant. Ranger was so interested watching him that he forgot to look for Nero the Hound. Perhaps he thought he was far enough from the Grand Old House to be safe. He did not think about the Playful Air Whiffs carrying his scent to Nero.

Ranger the Coyote did not see Nero until Nero was almost on him. Ranger started to run away, but it was too late. You should have seen what a thrashing Nero gave Ranger before he got away! Then Nero the Hound trotted back to the Grand

Old House as if he had done his duty, while Ranger the Coyote raced back to the hills where he could hide and lick the wounds that Nero's sharp teeth had made.

After that, Old Cluck and her Chicklets could feed in the Green Meadow in safety, for Ranger was glad to stay away.

That night Mrs. Smith gave Nero the Hound an extra good supper, for she had seen him drive Ranger away. She knew that if Nero had not been watching, Ranger the Coyote might have caught some of Old Cluck's Chicklets. So Nero was given an extra dish of mush and milk to pay him for his faithfulness.

CHAPTER 21

Spink the Bobolink Sings a Song

SOME time after Redwing the Blackbird moved into the Sheltered Little Cove, another neighbor arrived from the Sunny Southland. He was black, with a design made up of white, brown, and gray. He was smaller than Redwing, and the first time Bud Smith saw him he said: "Well, there is Spink the Bobolink back again."

Spink the Bobolink was really an interesting fellow. He was a first cousin of Redwing the Blackbird, and perhaps that is the reason why he liked the Marshy Banks along the Duck Pond as Redwing did. Spink was also a first cousin of Burlingame the Meadow Lark and Weaver the Oriole.

Spink had two suits that he wore on different occasions. He also had two names. The flashy spring suit that he was wearing when he came to the Duck Pond on the Old Homestead was the one he wore in the Northland. He always came north about two weeks ahead of Mrs. Bobolink; then all he had to do was sit around and sing.

When Mrs. Bobolink arrived, they built a nest on the ground in the Green Meadow, as their cousin Burlingame the Lark did, but not far from the Sheltered Little Cove. They were different from their other cousin, Weaver the Oriole, when it came to nest building, for he built his nest on a Springy Limb of the Big Elm that stood in the front yard by the Grand Old House.

Perhaps you would like to know about Spink's other suit and his other name before hearing more of his adventures on the Old Homestead. You see, Spink had lived at the Old Homestead two summers, for he had been hatched there two summers before.

When Spink got ready to go to the Sunny Southland to spend the winter, he changed his coat entirely. You would never have known he was the same bird. His coat was then quite plain, and he looked almost like Mrs. Bobolink in her modest yellowish-brown dress with a few trimmings of yellow and white. No, you would never have known Spink in that suit.

When he arrived in the Sunny Southland, he lived in the rice fields and ate so much rice that he grew fat. People in the Sunny Southland called him Ricebird because he ate so much rice, and he was not so well liked as he was in the Northland. For one thing, he was so busy eating rice that he even forgot to sing, and his drab coat surely was

"Spink the Bobolink is back again," said Bud.

not anything in his favor. It was a good thing for Spink that he went on to South America to spend the winter after he had eaten his fill of rice, for he had so many friends and they ate so much rice that they were a nuisance. Mr. Rice Grower sometimes lost his patience entirely, and killed many of Spink's friends.

But, my, what a different fellow was Spink the Bobolink when he came back to the Old Homestead! He put on his best suit like a regular dandy, and he sang from morning until night. There were not many of the Mallards' neighbors who could sing except Redwing the Blackbird and Spink the Bobolink. It would be hard to imagine the Spoonbills or Diver the Grebe or Longlegs the Heron or Jack Snipe or any of the others singing.

Yes, Redwing the Blackbird and Spink the Bobolink were about the best songsters at the Duck

(129)

Pond. They often met and sang a duet together. Sometimes it was in the Sheltered Little Cove, or among the Fuzzy Cattails along the Marshy Banks, and sometimes they met in the Green Meadow, or along Little River. Then Burlingame the Meadow Lark would add his song to theirs.

One day Spink the Bobolink did not appear for the regular concert.

"I wonder what has happened to Spink," said Redwing.

Then he saw Spink flying toward the Green Meadow with a Fat Grasshopper in his beak, and he knew that Spink was too busy feeding a family to sing.

It was not long until the Baby Bobolinks were able to fly, and then the whole family played around in the Green Meadow and along Little River and by the Duck Pond. Soon they joined another family and another until there was a large flock of them together.

Of course, Redwing's Wee Blackbirds had grown large also, and the Wee Blackbirds of Redwing's friends had grown large, so there was a large flock of blackbirds as well as bobolinks at the Duck Pond. And you should have heard those blackbirds sing!

But Spink the Bobolink was not doing much

singing any more. He was changing his clothes and getting ready to start for the Sunny Southland again. Perhaps he was thinking of the feasts he would have in the rice fields on his way to his winter home.

Spink would be ready to leave the Chilly Northland a long time ahead of the blackbirds and the bluebirds and many other of the Feathered Friends on the Old Homestead. That was because he traveled slower and stopped over in the rice fields to get fat before continuing his long journey to South America.

It was too bad that Spink and his friends had to make such pigs of themselves eating rice. It would have been all right if they had eaten what they needed and then had gone on. But Spink was not the same gentleman in the Sunny Southland that he was in the Land of Cool Breezes. He ate and ate and grew fatter and fatter until Fearful the Man came along and killed many of Spink's friends and ate them.

Chapter 22

Mr. Bluebird Visits the Duck Pond

MR. AND MRS. BLUEBIRD had built a nest in the Nesting Box that Bud Smith had made for them and set on an iron post in the front yard by the Grand Old House. Bud had used an iron post so that Hunting Cat could not climb up to the nest.

The Bluebirds had five babies to feed, and with Robin Red and Jenny Wren and Weaver the Oriole and others all hunting bugs and caterpillars and worms around the Grand Old House, it was quite a job for everyone to find enough.

One day Mr. Bluebird decided he would fly over to the Duck Pond. He thought perhaps it would be easier to find something there for the Baby Bluebirds to eat. He did not know that Redwing the Blackbird and Spink the Bobolink and Burlingame the Meadow Lark and many other Feathered Friends had been hunting around the Duck Pond and through the Green Meadow. All he knew was that he had to find something to feed to five Baby Bluebirds.

Of course, some people would not have called them "babies" any more. They were really almost grown, for they had grown feathers, and within a few days they would be ready to leave the nest. But my, how much they could eat!

While Mrs. Bluebird was looking for a Fat Grasshopper over by High Cliff, near where Molly and Peter lived, Mr. Bluebird flew across the Green Meadow to the Jungle Thicket by the Duck Pond and alighted on a Wild Berry Bush to look around.

Mr. Bluebird had been to the Duck Pond many times before. He and Mrs. Bluebird went to the Duck Pond and down along Little River in search of bugs and dried berries when they first came back to the Old Homestead from the Sunny Southland. Mr. Bluebird had arrived a week or two ahead of Mrs. Bluebird, when food was rather scarce, and he had hunted alone until she came.

After the Baby Bluebirds had been hatched, Mr. Bluebird had been too busy feeding them to go far from home. For that reason it had been quite a while since he had visited the Duck Pond. He was wondering who were living there that year. He liked the Duck Pond with its Marshy Banks and the Jungle Thicket on one side of it, but he liked it up by the Grand Old House better.

While Mr. Bluebird was looking around, he suddenly saw a movement on the ground. At first

Mr. and Mrs. Blue-
bird built a nest in the
Nesting Box by the
Grand Old House.

he thought it was a large worm crawling along.
Then he noticed that something was pushing up
the ground into a snakelike ridge. It seemed
strange to see the ground rise in all sorts of twists
and turns. Mr. Bluebird hopped down where he
could see it better.

"Now, what do you suppose is doing that?" said
Mr. Bluebird, as the little ridge grew longer.
"Sure-ly, sure-ly that is a strange sight."

Then, right while Mr. Bluebird was watching,
the ground broke through and out popped the
head of Miner the Mole.

Miner the Mole was a relative of Barney the
Shrew, who lived in the Woodshed by the Grand
Old House and ate the ants and sawflies that
fell out of the wood that Bud split. At first sight
both Barney and Miner looked something like

Whiskers the Mouse. But Barney and Miner did not have any ears that showed like Whiskers', and their eyes were not much better than none. Both of them had much longer noses than Whiskers had.

No, Miner's eyes were not much good. He worked underground so much that he had little use for eyes. Sometimes at night, when the light was not strong enough to hurt his eyes, Miner came to the surface to hunt. That was usually on wet nights when the Wriggly Earthworms came to the surface. Miner surely was fond of Wriggly Earthworms.

When Miner's nose appeared above ground, he was not quite sure whether it would be safe to show his head or not. He could not see, and did not know if enemies were near.

While Mr. Bluebird was watching, the ground broke through and out popped Miner the Mole.

Mr. Bluebird was much interested in Miner the Mole. He wondered what Miner had been doing under the ground out of sight.

"Hello, Mr. Mole," said Mr. Bluebird. "You seem to be busy today."

Now, Mr. Bluebird probably did not know it, but Miner the Mole was almost always busy. It was not uncommon for him to dig a hundred feet of Secret Tunnels in a day and a night. It seemed as if Miner never rested and slept.

Miner the Mole was ready to pull back his head and go on with his work when he heard Mr. Bluebird. "Yes, I am busy," he said; "but who are you?"

"I am Mr. Bluebird, and I live in a Nesting Box up by the Grand Old House."

Of course Miner the Mole did not know anything about the Grand Old House, and he did not know much about anything. He lived underground so much that almost everything was new and strange to him.

"And what is the Grand Old House?" he asked.

"That is the home of Bud and Mary Smith," replied Mr. Bluebird. "Bud built my Nesting Box for me."

"How far is it to the Grand Old House?" asked Miner.

"Oh, it is only a little way," said Mr. Bluebird. "It is across the Green Meadow."

Mr. Bluebird did not realize that what seemed a short distance for him to fly would be a long, long way for Miner the Mole to dig. It would be like a man in an automobile telling a man who was walking that it was a short distance to town. But Mr. Bluebird did not intend to fool Miner.

Saw-Whet the Owl Is Disappointed

MR. BLUEBIRD was so interested visiting with Miner the Mole that he did not remember he had come after something to feed to the Baby Bluebirds, and Miner the Mole was so interested hearing about the Great Wide World that he stopped his work for a visit.

There was Mr. Bluebird, who had been many places and had seen many wonderful things, but who did not know anything about the Underground World where Miner lived. There was Miner the Mole, who knew many things about his Underground World, but who knew little about the Great Wide World. All Miner knew was that the Great Wide World was filled with Flying Enemies and Walking Enemies that pounced upon his friends whenever they showed themselves above ground, and that he had to be careful where he went.

"Why are you digging so many Secret Tunnels here by the Duck Pond?" asked Mr. Bluebird. Then Miner the Mole told Mr. Bluebird some interesting things about his Underground World. Said Miner the Mole: "I have been living down in what you call the Green Meadow. There are usually plenty of Wriggly Earthworms there for me to eat. But when the ground becomes dry and hard because there has been no rain, it is hard for me to dig. So I move here by the Duck Pond where the ground is moist and soft. Even the Wriggly Earthworms like the moist ground, and some of them who are not too far away move here."

"Why do you need so many Secret Tunnels?" asked Mr. Bluebird.

"Those are my Hunting Tunnels," said Miner the Mole. "I run through them when I hunt, instead of walking above ground. Then my enemies cannot see me. Sometimes I find Wriggly Earthworms and Cutworms and Grubs and Bugs in them. They walk in my Hunting Tunnels where they will not be seen by their enemies in the Great Wide World."

"It is all the fault of Satchelface the Pocket Gopher," said Miner to Mr. Bluebird.

"Don't you get lonesome working in your Hunting Tunnels all alone?" asked Mr. Bluebird. "I should think you would want company."

"Oh, no," replied Miner, "because, you see, I am not alone. Sometimes there are more than twenty of us who are using the same Hunting Tunnels, and, of course, we meet quite often. We join our Hunting Tunnels, and then have plenty of company. But we are not always safe even though we stay out of sight. Sometimes Digger the Badger comes along, and then we have quite a time to escape. Sometimes Reddy Fox and even Nero the Hound dig after us."

"And I suppose that Forktongue the Snake tries to catch you in your Hunting Tunnels," said Mr. Bluebird.

"Yes, he does. But one of our greatest enemies is Fearful the Man. You see, it is all the fault of Satchelface the Pocket Gopher. Whenever Satchelface finds where Fearful the Man has planted his crops, he burrows along the row and eats the Sprouting Little Seeds. That makes Fearful the Man angry. Sometimes we also find where Fearful has planted his crops. Wherever there are Sprouting Little Seeds, we know that there are sure to be Cutworms and Grubs to eat them. Then we dig Hunting Tunnels along the rows of

"Ho-hum," said Saw-Whet the Owl
sleepily. "It's about time to look for
a Tender Mouse to eat."

Sprouting Little Seeds so we can catch the Cutworms and the Grubs. But when Fearful the Man
sees our Hunting Tunnels along his Sprouting
Little Seeds, he thinks Satchelface has been help-
ing himself to his crops. Then Fearful sets traps
in our Hunting Tunnels. I do wish that someone
would tell Fearful that we are trying to help him
by ridding his garden of Cutworms and Grubs.

"I think Fearful the Man should be more careful," said Mr. Bluebird.

"Sometimes Trapper Jim also sets traps for us,"
said Miner. "Danny Muskrat told me once that
Trapper Jim also sets traps for him. He said he
heard Trapper Jim say that furs were a good price,
and that he could even sell moleskins now."

While Mr. Bluebird was listening to Miner the
Mole, the Long Shadows had been creeping across

(141)

the Old Homestead, and Saw-Whet the Owl had awakened from his all-day sleep.

"Ho-hum, ho-hum," he said sleepily. "It's about time to look for a Tender Mouse to eat."

He flitted through the treetops and alighted on a limb not far from where Mr. Bluebird and Miner the Mole were visiting. It was not yet quite dark enough for him to see well. Saw-Whet the Owl was timid, and he never came out until after dark. But Saw-Whet was quite sure that he saw a Tender Mouse on the ground, and he came a little nearer.

Sure enough, he could see a ball of silky gray fur sitting up and squeaking like everything. It was Miner the Mole telling his troubles to Mr. Bluebird. Miner had entirely forgotten to watch for enemies. But Mr. Bluebird's bright eyes had seen Saw-Whet the Owl.

Saw-Whet thought that Miner the Mole was a Tender Mouse. Of course, if he had known it was Miner, it would have made no difference. A mole would have tasted as good to Saw-Whet as would a Tender Mouse. So Saw-Whet was all ready to drop down and grab Miner.

"An enemy, an enemy," warned Mr. Bluebird, as he darted away toward the Nesting Box near the Grand Old House.

Miner the Mole did not wait to see which enemy was near. He ducked into his Hunting Tunnel almost before you could wink an eye, and Saw-Whet the Owl sat there looking at a hole in the ground.

What do you suppose Mrs. Bluebird said when Mr. Bluebird returned without a Fat Grasshopper?

CHAPTER 24

Bud Smith Sets a Trap

IT was a hot day in August. The Fluffy Ducklets had awakened from sleeping in the shade
of a Drooping Willow Tree that grew along the
Marshy Bank of the Duck Pond. But you would
never have known they were the same Fluffy
Ducklets that belonged to Mr. and Mrs. Mallard.
Each one had put on a beautiful new coat of
feathers, and it would have been hard to tell them
from Mr. and Mrs. Mallard at a distance They
were almost the size of their parents.

"Let's go for a swim," suggested Ducky Diver;
"it is so hot here on the bank."

"Qua-ack quack-quack-quack," said Mrs. Mallard, and she started toward the water, followed
by the others. "I do believe it would be cooler in
the water."

Soon all the Mallards were splashing and diving
and having a fine time playing Tip-up. Whenever they saw something in the Oozy Mud on the
bottom of the Duck Pond that they could not reach
by playing Tip-up, then they would play Dive.
Down they would go to the bottom out of sight,
and then they would come up some other place.

Tip-up and Dive were the two games they liked to play.

But the Young Mallards had learned another game that they liked quite as well. It was the game of Sail. You see, they had grown strong wings, and they no longer had to swim across the Duck Pond unless they wanted to. If they wished, they could fly.

Sometimes when they became tired of playing Tip-up and Dive on one side of the Duck Pond, they would play Sail over to the other side. Then they would play Tip-up and Dive again. What a good time they had!

After they had splashed and ducked and dived for a while on that August day, Ducky Doodles became restless. He wanted a change. "Let's play Sail over to the other side," he said.

In a moment all the Mallards were in the air. But instead of playing Sail straight across the Duck Pond, Mr. Mallard led them higher and higher. Soon they were playing Sail around and around high above the water. At last when their young wings began to get tired, Mr. Mallard set his wings and sailed gracefully down to the Duck Pond, followed by the Young Mallards.

"Oh, wasn't that fun!" exclaimed Ducky Waddles.

"Let's do it again when we go back to the other side," said Ducky Doodles.

"Yes, let's," said Ducky Diver.

Now, it happened that when the Mallards were playing Sail high above the water Bud Smith was watching them from the front gate by the Grand Old House. And Mary had seen them from the Fragrant Flower Garden, where she was gathering a bouquet of marigolds.

"Oh, did you see the Mallards?" asked Mary, as she came running toward Bud. "They were playing Sail high above the water."

"Yes, I saw them," replied Bud. "I suppose they are exercising their wings so that they will be strong enough to carry them to the Sunny Southland one of these days. It will not be long until Jack Frost will start to paint the Dancing Little

"Oh, did you see the Mallards?" asked Mary. "They were playing Sail high above the water."

Leaflets, and then Old Man Winter will be here again. Why, school will start again in two weeks."

"I wish the Mallards didn't have to leave," said Mary. "But I suppose they can't be expected to stay here after the Duck Pond is frozen over."

"No, I suppose not," said Bud.

Bud was thoughtful as he turned and walked back toward the Grand Old House. The next day he came out to the mailbox carrying a letter. It was addressed to the Bureau of Biological Survey, Department of Agriculture, Washington, D. C.

Some days later a mysterious package and a letter in a long envelope were left by the mail carrier. They were addressed to Bud, and came from the Bureau of Biological Survey.

"Now, what are you getting from the Government?" asked Mary.

Bud smiled and said nothing as he hurried up to his room. That afternoon Mary heard the sound of a hammer and a saw in the Workshop, and when she entered the door she found Bud covering a large, queer-looking, open-bottomed cage with fine chicken wire.

"What's that?" asked Mary.

"Wait and see," teased Bud, as he drove a staple into place. In the back of the cage Bud had built a small door, and over this door he had fitted a smaller cage that was covered on the bottom as well as the sides. This cage also had a door in it into which Bud could put his hand.

"I'll bet that's a trap," said Mary, hoping to get Bud to say something that would betray his secret.

"Wait and see," said Bud with a smile, and he drove in another staple.

"You're not going to trap the Mallards, are you?" asked Mary.

"Yes, of course I am," said Bud.

Mary thought Bud was fooling her. "Truly now, what are you going to use that thing for—a rabbit hutch?"

"I told you," said Bud. "I am going to trap the Mallards in it."

"But you are joking about that."

"No, I mean it," said Bud.

"Bud Smith, what are you going to do with those Mallards?"

"You wait and see," laughed Bud.

"How long must I wait?"

"Until tomorrow," said Bud, and he resumed his hammering.

CHAPTER 25

The Mallards Are Caught

THE next morning Bud started to the Duck
Pond with his Big Cage Trap. Besides the
trap he carried a long piece of stout cord such as
Farmer Smith used for binding the Golden Yellow Grain into bundles. He also took along a large
pocketful of corn and the mysterious package that
had arrived through the mail.

"I am going with you," announced Mary, as
Bud started across the Green Meadow.

"All right, you may come if you like," said Bud.

Bud let Mary help him carry the Big Cage Trap
to the Duck Pond, for it really was too large for
him to manage well alone.

"You are not going to kill the Mallards or keep
them prisoners, are you?" asked Mary as they
walked along.

"There you go asking questions again," replied
Bud. "What difference does it make?"

"If you try to keep them prisoners, I'll turn them
loose; and if you're going to kill them, I'll stand
on the bank all day and shoo them away from your
trap; so there," said Mary.

"I'm not going to kill them, and I'm not going

(149)

It was the place where
the Mallards always came out on the bank
when they were tired of swimming.

to keep them more than a few minutes," promised
Bud, when he thought that Mary might interfere.

"Then what do you want to trap them for?"

"You wait a little while and I'll show you."

"Well, I suppose if I have to, I can; but I warn
you not to hurt them."

Bud and Mary carried the Big Cage Trap to a
place on the Marshy Bank of the Duck Pond
where they had often seen the Mallards sunning
themselves. It was the place where the Mallards
always came out on the bank when they were tired
of swimming, that is, if a duck ever gets tired
of such sport.

When the Big Cage Trap was placed where
Bud wanted it, he cut a short stick and propped up

one side high enough so the Mallards could walk under it. He tied one end of his long string to the top of the prop, and unwound the rest of it until it reached to a large clump of Tumbled Bulrushes.

"You sit here out of sight while I go back and scatter the corn," said Bud to Mary.

Bud scattered some of the corn on the ground in front of the Big Cage Trap, but most of it he placed under it.

"Pull the string and see how it works," he called to Mary. Mary gave the string a pull and down came the front of the Big Cage Trap.

"That's good," said Bud; "now wait till I set it again."

Bud propped up the front of the Big Cage Trap as he had done the first time, covered it with a few Fuzzy Cattails to partly hide it, and then hid himself in the big clump of Tumbled Bulrushes beside Mary.

"I guess the Mallards must be over in the Sheltered Little Cove," said Bud, "but they will be back here before long."

"I hope they come soon," said Mary.

Bud cut a few Fuzzy Cattails and stuck them around to fill some openings in the Tumbled Bulrushes. He was afraid the sharp eyes of the Mallards might look through the openings and see

Mary and him. Then he put some over the top so the Mallards could not see them if they flew over.

After a while Mary grew tired of waiting. "I wish they would hurry," she said. Bud and Mary had not been waiting long, but it seemed like a long time to Mary.

Suddenly Mary pointed across the Duck Pond. "Oh, look! There they come."

"Psst," whispered Bud. "Not so loud. Keep down or they will see you. Don't try to watch them, or you will scare them away. I'll do the watching."

"I want to see them," said Mary.

"Here, stick some of this Swamp Grass in your hair; that will help to hide it," said Bud, and he put a few pieces in his cap.

On came the Mallards. When they were near shore, they stopped to play Tip-up and Dive awhile. Mary's heart was jumping, and once she almost caused Bud to pull the string. Some of the Mallards were swimming nearer to shore.

"Quiet down before you spoil everything," whispered Bud; "you are shaking as if you were cold."

"I can't help it," said Mary. "I'm afraid they won't go under."

Of course, the Mallards had no idea that Bud had set a Big Cage Trap for them. They thought everything looked the same as when they had left. They had not looked closely, because they were so used to finding everything the same when they came back to sit on the Marshy Bank.

At last Mrs. Mallard walked up the bank. She noticed a few grains of corn lying there, and she ate them. A little farther she saw some more, and she walked over and ate them.

"Qua-ack quack-quack-quack," said Mrs. Mallard. "Look at all the corn I have found."

It didn't take the rest of the Mallards long to scramble out of the water and up the bank, and soon all of them were scooping up corn with their broad bills.

Bud gave the string a quick pull, and down came the Big Cage Trap.

"Oh, goody!" said Mary, "we caught every one."

"Say, that was luck," said Bud; "I didn't expect to get more than half of them the first time. Go easy so as not to frighten them until they get used to us. They might fly against the Big Cage Trap and hurt themselves."

"I wonder what Mrs. Mallard is saying to her youngsters," said Mary; "they must be terribly scared."

CHAPTER 26

A New Experience for the Mallards

OF course when the Mallards first learned
that they were prisoners they were frightened. They could not understand what had happened. Bud and Mary approached the Big Cage
Trap quietly so as not to alarm them. The
Mallards ran into the small cage at the back, and
Bud closed the door between.

"Well, now that you have them caught what
are you going to do with them?" asked Mary.

"Band them," said Bud, as he took the mysterious package from his pocket.

"What do you mean?" asked Mary.

Bud opened the box. In it were a number of
small, aluminum bands with numbers on them.
"We'll put a band on a leg of each one, and then
we'll know if they come back to the Duck Pond
next summer."

"How interesting!" said Mary. "So that is what
you got from the Government."

"Yes; you see we must get a permit from the
Government before we can band birds. Then
when we put a band on a bird, we make out a card
saying what kind of bird we put it on, where and

when we banded it, and such things, and send it to Washington. These cards are kept on file, and if the birds are ever caught again, the Government knows how far they are from the place where they were banded."

Bud reached his hand into the cage and brought out one of the Mallards. After a band had been put on its leg, Bud wrote the number of the band on a card, and put the duck back into the big cage. Then he finished filling out the card with the information that was wanted.

One by one the Mallards were banded in the same way and placed in the large cage until at last Bud came to Mr. Mallard himself. "Oh, see here!" exclaimed Bud. "Mr. Mallard is already wearing a band. Now, where do you suppose he got it? We must send the number to Washington and find out. Let's see, it is 96,501. I'm anxious to find out where Mr. Mallard was before he came here."

Bud wrote the number on a piece of paper, and put Mr. Mallard in with the rest of his family. Then after all of them had been banded, Bud raised the Big Cage Trap, and away flew the Mallards.

"Let us see if we can catch the Spoonbills, also," suggested Mary.

"I haven't any more corn with me," said Bud; "but we can come back tomorrow and try it. We can leave the Big Cage Trap hidden in the Jungle Thicket."

Bud and Mary carried the Big Cage Trap into the Jungle Thicket, and then started back to the Grand Old House.

"How did you know about banding birds?" asked Mary, as they walked along.

"I thought it would be nice if some of our Feathered Friends on the Old Homestead were marked so that we would know them if they came back next year. That night after we saw the Mallards playing Sail I asked Dad about it, and he said he would write to the Biological Survey for me. It is too late to do much this year, but next year I intend to have some different kinds of Cage Traps ready and start early, because the Fish and Wildlife Service has asked us to start a banding station on the Old Homestead."

Robin Red's family
had already left
the nest.

"Yes, I suppose it is a little late to do much this year," said Mary. "The Bluebirds have gone to the Big Mountains where it is cooler, and the Robins and Orioles and Kingbirds have left their nests, also. But it will be fun to band the Spoonbills."

"I am going to write to Washington and send the number of Mr. Mallard's band," said Bud, when they arrived at the Grand Old House. And this is what Bud wrote:

"DEAR SIRS:

"I received the bird bands that you sent to me, and today when I was putting them on the Mallards I found that Mr. Mallard already had a band on his leg. It was No. 96,501. I wonder where this was put on and when, and also who did it. I am going to try to put bands on the Spoonbills tomorrow, and then I will send all the file cards to you which you sent. Next year I want to put bands on lots of birds, but school starts next week and you know how much time that leaves a fellow. I hope you will not forget to tell me who banded Mr. Mallard.   "Yours truly,

"BUD SMITH."

A few days later, Bud received an answer to his letter, which read:

"DEAR BUD:

"Your letter in which you gave us the number of a band that you found on the leg of an adult male mallard has been received, for which we thank you.

"You will probably be interested to know that this duck was banded two years ago this fall at Thomasville, Georgia, by C. T. James.

"We hope that you will report the progress of your work from time to time, and we know you will find it interesting.

"Very truly yours,
"FISH AND WILDLIFE SERVICE."

"How far Mr. Mallard has traveled!" said Mary, when Bud read the letter to her.

"Yes, and not once but several times," replied Bud. "You see, he was banded two years ago, and that means he has made three trips since then between the Sunny Southland and the Land of Cool Breezes."

"Oh, I do hope that the Mallards come back to the Old Homestead next spring," said Mary.

CHAPTER 27

A Visit With Sandhill the Crane

YOU may be sure that the Young Mallards were glad to get away when Bud lifted the Big Cage Trap and turned them loose. They did not quite know what to think about it. Of course, Mr. Mallard had been banded before, but still he was not sure what Bud would do. A duck can never be sure what Fearful the Man will do, or what Fearful the Man's boy will do. So the Mallards flew to the Yellow Stubble Field to talk it over. They thought they would be safe there.

The Yellow Stubble Field was a long way from the Duck Pond. Farmer Smith had gathered the Golden Yellow Grain long before, but there were still many, many Tempting Kernels on the ground that had fallen out of the heads.

In a little while the Mallards were so busy hunting Tempting Kernels that they were too interested to think about the Big Cage Trap and their fright. They waddled about among the Yellow Stubbles and quacked their delight to one another.

Finally Ducky Doodles looked up at the sky. He had heard a queer call from someone up there, which he had never heard before. "Carrrrrump,

"Those birds are Sandhill the Crane and his friends,"
said Mrs. Mallard to Ducky Doodles.

carrrrrump," it sounded far above. Then Ducky Doodles saw a flock of strange birds, with long necks sticking out in front and long legs sticking out behind. They were playing a game of Sail, and they scarcely moved their wings. Ducky Doodles did not know whether they were friends or enemies. He was afraid they might swoop down like Sharptoes the Duck Hawk and carry away some of his brothers and sisters.

"Oh, what are those strange birds up there?" asked Ducky Doodles.

"Those are Sandhill the Crane and his friends," said Mrs. Mallard.

"Where are they going, Mother?" asked Ducky Diver.

(160)

"They are going back to the Sunny Southland before Old Man Winter comes down from the Land of Ice. I suppose Sandhill the Crane is all tired out and hungry after playing the game of Sail all day. Perhaps he would like to stop and eat some of the Tempting Kernels," and Mrs. Mallard quacked as loud as she could to let Sandhill know that the Yellow Stubble Field was a good place to stop.

Sandhill the Crane heard, and began to sail in a wide circle, followed by his friends. Sandhill was old and wise. He knew that sometimes Terror the Hunter put out wooden ducks and geese in the field to fool him, and used a coarse reed on which he quacked like a duck. The wooden decoys looked so much like live ducks that it was difficult for even Sandhill the Crane to tell the difference. He wanted to be sure.

So Sandhill was not in any hurry to settle down in the Yellow Stubble Field even though he was hungry. Around and around sailed the Cranes, spying out every place where Terror the Hunter might be hidden.

"Qua-ack quack-quack-quack," said Mrs. Mallard. "Come on down. There is no danger here, and there are plenty of Tempting Kernels."

"Carrrrrump, carrrrrump," said Sandhill the

Crane. "Are you sure Terror the Hunter is not hiding near?"

"Yes, I am sure," said Mrs. Mallard.

At last Sandhill the Crane and his friends floated down and settled in the Yellow Stubble Field near the Mallards. But Sandhill was not to be caught napping. Whenever he stopped to eat he always posted sentinels to watch for Terror the Hunter. He had learned that it paid to be careful.

Mr. and Mrs. Mallard knew that Sandhill the Crane was one bird that Terror the Hunter could not creep up on easily. You see, Sandhill was tall. He was almost as tall as Longlegs the Heron, and Longlegs was almost as tall as Bud. Sandhill could see a long way because he was so tall, and the Mallards felt quite safe when he was near with his sentinels.

Sandhill the Crane was one of the first of the Feathered Friends to leave the Chilly Northland before Old Man Winter came down from the Land of Ice and covered the Great Wide World with a Soft White Blanket. Perhaps it was because Sandhill's long neck and legs got cold so easily that he came early. The Mallards knew that when he appeared it would soon be time for them to start for the Sunny Southland. Of course the Mallards did not mind the cold so much, because they had thick, warm coats of Glossy Feathers; but they did mind it when the water froze over.

The Mallards were having a fine time, when suddenly one of Sandhill's sentinels sounded an alarm.

"Carrrrrump, carrrrrump," he said. "I see something that looks suspicious."

Then all Sandhill's friends stopped eating and looked. Sure enough, there was something dark on the edge of the field, and Sandhill decided it was time to go.

"Carrrrrump, carrrrrump," called Sandhill as he took to the air. And the Mallards did not waste any time getting back to the Duck Pond.

"What do you suppose Sandhill the Crane saw?" asked Ducky Diver, after the Mallards had reached the Duck Pond. "I did not see anything."

Whenever Sandhill stopped to eat, he always posted sentinels to watch for Terror the Hunter.

"That is because you are young, and your eyes are not yet trained to look for danger," said Mr. Mallard. "When you are as old as Sandhill the Crane, you will be able to see many things that you do not now notice."

"Shall we see Sandhill again?" asked Ducky Doodles.

"Perhaps we shall see him in the Sunny Southland," said Mr. Mallard, "for he lives near us during the winter. We shall also meet many other Feathered Friends who have been spending their summer in the Chilly Northland."

CHAPTER 28

Honker the Goose Takes a Rest

HONKER the Goose left the Land of Cool Breezes one day late in September. He had with him his family and some of his friends. He had lived all summer in the Chilly Northland, where Mrs. Goose had built a nest near a lake and had raised six fine Goslings.

There had been a time during the summer when Honker the Goose and the other geese could not fly. You see, Honker wore a heavy coat of Glossy Feathers; and when the warm summer days came, he was too warm. So Honker had lost most of his feathers, including many from his wings; and for a while he had not enough to carry him. He lived on the ground and on the water then, and if danger came near he had to run away or hide. If he was on the water, he frequently dove out of sight and swam to the Tumbled Bulrushes to hide.

As the Playful Air Whiffs grew colder and colder, Honker's feathers grew in again, and by fall, when the Fat Goslings had grown their Glossy Feathers, Honker had also put on a bright new coat and was ready to fly again.

One late September day Honker called his family and some of his friends together and told them it was time to start for the Sunny Southland. Honker was in the lead, and behind him, in two long rows that made a large V in the sky, followed the others. Honker was strong and wise, and he flew ahead of the others to guide them on the long journey, so they would be sure not to lose the way.

Sometimes when Honker grew tired he would drop back into one of the lines and one of his strong friends would take his place at the head of the big V. Sandhill the Crane and his friends had already started for the Sunny Southland about three weeks before; but then Sandhill always started ahead of almost everyone else.

One day, while Honker and his flock were flying southward, the Gray Cloud Ships came sailing across the sky and the Merry Little Snowflakes began to fall. It was rather confusing to know where to fly when Honker could not see the way; so, as the Weird Darkness began to steal over the Great Wide World, Honker guided his flock downward in search of a Resting Place.

"Honk-honk," said Honker the Goose as a signal, and "Honk, honk, honk," answered the others all along the lines. Then the lines tipped

The next morning the Laughing Yellow Sun came out.

downward, and soon Honker and his friends were skimming along not far above the ground.

Suddenly, in the Weird Darkness, Honker saw a small patch of water. "Qua-ack quack-quack-quack," called someone from below, and Honker turned his flock and flew back over the water.

Honker was tired, and his friends and family were tired, and Honker did not spend so much time as he usually did in spying out the land before coming down. It was getting late, and it would be hard to find another Resting Place.

Honker circled again and started back toward the water. Then he saw the Grand Old House. That was not the first time he had seen it, for Honker had made many trips. "It is the Old Homestead," said Honker, as he set his wings to

glide down to the Duck Pond. "I know we shall
be safe here."

My, what a quacking and a honking there was
as Honker and his flock plunked into the water
near the Mallards! Even Bud heard it up at the
Grand Old House as he carried in the last armful
of wood for the night.

"Honker and his friends are back," said Bud, as
he piled the wood in the wood box, "and you
should hear what a noise they are making with
the Mallards."

"It's a sure sign that Old Man Winter has arrived when Honker the Goose goes south," said
Farmer Smith.

But the next morning the Laughing Yellow Sun
came out, and for a week Honker and his flock did
not leave. Each morning, about the time that the
Smiling Yellow Sun was peeping out of the east,
Honker would take his family to the Rustling
Cornfield for breakfast. When they were full, they
would fly back to the Duck Pond for a game of
Tip-up until afternoon. Then back to the Rustling
Cornfield they would go for supper, and at dark
they would return to the Duck Pond for the night.

Of course, the Mallards were enjoying trips to
the Rustling Cornfield also, and sometimes they
went to the Yellow Stubble Field for a change.

For some reason Honker always liked to go back to the same place.

One day Terror the Hunter noticed that Honker always took his family to the same place to feed. So he thought he would hide in the Rustling Cornfield and get a goose when the flock came there for breakfast. But Honker was a wise old leader. He had been expecting Terror to do that very thing, and he was watching. He was not going to be caught off guard at any time.

That morning Honker noticed a bright flash as he circled over the field with his followers. The Laughing Yellow Sun had flashed a warning reflection to Honker from Terror's shining gun, and Honker took his family to another place for breakfast. Then, instead of going back to the Duck

Honker took his family to the Rustling Cornfield for breakfast.

Pond, he led them far, far to the southward toward their winter home.

"Honker the Goose has left," said Bud that night; "we must be going to have another storm."

Of course, Bud did not know that Honker the Goose had been alarmed by Terror the Hunter. He thought Honker had left because a storm was coming; for Honker usually played Sail ahead of storms. Perhaps Honker left because he really did know a storm was on the way, but he had been frightened by Terror the Hunter, also. It was strange how Honker could tell when the Merry Little Snowflakes were about to fall, but many of the Wild Creatures can do that.

CHAPTER 29

The Young Mallards Hear a Story

IT was a gray day at the Old Homestead the day after Honker the Goose left with his family. As Bud had guessed, a storm was threatening.

The Mallards sat huddled on the Marshy Bank of the Duck Pond, but the Marshy Bank was no longer soft. The Drooping Willow Trees were leafless, and the Tumbled Bulrushes were tan instead of green. Most of the Feathered Friends had left.

Over among the Fuzzy Cattails Danny Muskrat was busy piling more Swamp Grass and Moss and Oozy Mud on his Grassy House to make it warmer. Of course the mud soon froze, but Danny did not mind that. There was a ring of ice around his Grassy House, and it would not be long until the Duck Pond would all be frozen over.

Each night the Playful Air Whiffs had grown colder, and each morning the ice along the Marshy Bank of the Duck Pond had grown thicker. Danny had expected that when he built his Grassy House. He had made his doorway so deep under water that it never froze. Danny could always leave his Grassy House through his underwater doorway; and after the Duck Pond was frozen over, he could stay under the ice.

As the nights grew colder, Danny Muskrat stayed more and more under the water. Instead of crawling out on the bank to eat his Juicy Water Bulbs and Sweet Cattail Stalks, he sat in the water or carried them inside his Grassy House to eat them. That was because every time he left the water, Jack Frost began to make Sharp Little Icicles on his fur.

It was queer how Danny could play under the ice after the Duck Pond froze over. First Danny would take a deep breath of air before he left his Grassy House. Danny could hold his breath a long, long time. After he had swum as long as he could hold his breath, he would come up under the

"The Sunny Southland is sometimes called the Land of Sunshine," said Mrs. Mallard. "It has many Swampy Lakes and Boggy Rivers in which to play."

ice. If he did not find an air pocket, he would let out his breath against the ice like a big bubble. Soon the air would be fresh, and Danny would take it into his lungs again and go on.

Down along Little River where the water was moving it did not freeze so easily. Sometimes the Mallards went there for a swim and a game of Tip-up in the Quiet Pools where the water was not so swift.

But the next day after Honker the Goose and his family left, the Mallards were sitting on the Marshy Bank of the Duck Pond, while Gray Cloud Ships scurried past overhead. They had gone to the Rustling Cornfield for breakfast, and there was nothing else to do but to sit.

At last Mr. Mallard began to tell the Young Mallards a story. It was about the time when he was as young and as inexperienced as they were.

"One day when I was young," he said, "my father called all his family together and said it was time to start for the Sunny Southland. Of course we did not know anything about the Sunny South-land, and we did not know anything about playing Sail so far. Father told us if we would always stay near him and do as he told us, we would never get into trouble.

"But one day we met some other young ducks

In the Rustling Cornfield they met another flock of
mallards, some of their friends who had
come northward with them in the spring.

who were going to the Sunny Southland. We
thought it would be fun to fly with them. So we
left our parents a little way and flew with the
young ducks awhile.

"The next day we left our parents a little farther,
and the first we knew we were so far away we
could not find them. When we arrived in the
Sunny Southland, there were but three of us left;
for, without our father to guide us, we had fallen
into many traps that Terror the Hunter had set for
us. That is what happens to all ducklets who
think they know better than their parents. You
must remember to stay with me.

"Soon we shall be starting for the Sunny Southland ourselves. I cannot tell you about all the

dangers, for they are too many. If you will stay with me, I can help you."

"Oh, tell us about the Sunny Southland," said Ducky Waddles.

"Yes, do," urged Ducky Doodles.

"Sometimes it is called the Land of Sunshine," said Mr. Mallard. "It lies far, far away, over many fields and lakes and rivers. It has many Swampy Lakes and Boggy Rivers in which to play, and it is near the Billowy Ocean. Almost all the Feathered Friends like to live there during Old Man Winter's reign in the Chilly Northland, because Jack Frost never comes near to nip the Tender Green Things and drive away the Crawly Bugs. So there is always plenty to eat.

"No, sir; Jack Frost knows better than to visit the Sunny Southland. He knows that the Laughing Yellow Sun would soon spoil all his fancywork if he did. But we must fly out to the Rustling Cornfield now and get our supper. It looks as if we would have a stormy night, and we must get back to the Duck Pond early."

Away flew the Mallards after what was to be their last meal on the Old Homestead that year.

In the Rustling Cornfield they met another flock of mallards. It was some of their friends who had come northward with them in the spring when Mr. Mallard had been wounded. Their friends had their own families with them, and soon they were all having a fine time together.

"You must stay with us on the Duck Pond tonight," said Mrs. Mallard to their friends, when they had finished their supper. So they all left the Rustling Cornfield together.

CHAPTER 30

"Good-by, Old Homestead"

WHEN the Mallards returned to the Duck Pond, it was snowing furiously. The Merry Little Snowflakes were dancing down and whirling in all directions. Already a Soft White Blanket covered everything. At last the storm that had been threatening all day had arrived.

In came the Mallards from the Rustling Cornfield and landed plump in the middle of the Duck Pond.

"I think we shall stay right here tonight," said Mr. Mallard. "We can draw our feet into our feathers, tuck our bills under our wings, and go right to sleep after we have had a drink. Then we do not need to fear Reddy Fox or Snoop the Weasel or Trailer the Mink. It will be much nicer than sitting in the snow all night on the Marshy Bank."

But the Young Mallards were not ready to go to sleep. They quacked and splashed and had a fine time. It was only the second snow they had ever seen, and they thought it was jolly fun.

"Listen to those Mallards tonight," said Bud to Mary; "they must be getting ready to leave."

"Oh, isn't this fun!" said Mary. "Tomorrow

after school we can go sliding on the Long Hill, and it will not be long until we can go skating on the Duck Pond."

That was a busy night for the Furry Friends on the Old Homestead. Reddy Fox was out looking for Molly Cottontail; but Molly was safe at home in her Friendly Burrow in the Little Jungle Thicket at the foot of High Cliff. Ranger the Coyote was hunting for Jack the Jumper; but Jack had made a Cozy Form in the Rustling Cornfield.

Snoop the Weasel was nosing around the Chicken House in his new, white winter coat; but Bud had been careful to see that he could not get in. Trailer the Mink and Lutra the Otter were both exploring along Little River. Billy Coon was sound asleep in his Hollow Den Tree, and Johnny

"Qua-ack quack-quack-quack," said Mrs. Mallard, which was her way of saying, "Good-by, Old Homestead."

Chuck was also asleep in his Hidden Den under a big rock on the side of High Cliff not far from where Molly and Peter lived. Digger the Badger was another sleepyhead, and so was Tawny Chipmunk.

Mephitis the Skunk was having the hardest time of all. He was looking for a Hidden Den where he could spend the winter with six or eight of his friends. You see, Mephitis liked to sleep with several in the same bed so he could keep warm. He hoped to find a Hidden Den in which some of his friends had already made a Grassy Bed and were snoozing. Then he could crawl right in and not have to make a bed himself. Of course Mephitis did not sleep all winter like Tawny Chipmunk. On nice warm nights Mephitis liked to take a short stroll to see if he could find Tiny the Meadow Mouse in the Rustling Corn Shocks.

Then there was Worker the Gray Squirrel and his thieving cousin, Chatterer the Red Squirrel. They did not care how much it snowed, for they had wisely provided a supply of cones and nuts and Tempting Kernels in their Secret Storehouses.

Virginia Opossum did not worry about cold weather in her Warm Hollow Log. She could sleep until warm days came again.

Hunting Cat lay sleeping on the Broad Hearth

in the Grand Old House, dreaming about catching Whiskers the Mouse. Nero the Hound was enjoying a warm bed in his new house that Bud had finished that day.

"Let's pop some corn and get out some apples and play it is Christmas," said Mary, as Bud threw down an armful of wood by the Glowing Fireplace.

"All right," agreed Bud. "Then we will ask Dad and Mother each to tell us a story."

The next morning was clear and cold, and the Laughing Yellow Sun had a time to make himself felt. The ice had crept inward toward the Mallards until only a small space remained open where they had stirred up the water during the night. The Rustling Cornfield and the Yellow Stubble Field were covered deeply with a Soft White Blanket, and it would have been a hard matter to find any Tempting Kernels.

Up at the Grand Old House Bud was scooping many pathways through the deep snow.

"I must take some grain out to Bobby White and the other Feathered Friends," he said to Mary, "for they cannot find any today."

"And I will take some alfalfa over to the Little Jungle Thicket for Molly and Peter. Then they will not have to leave their Friendly Burrow to hunt for food; if they did, Ranger the Coyote might catch them," said Mary.

"We must hurry or we shall be late to school," said Bud. "I have to carry in some wood for Mother before I leave."

"And some water," added Mary.

High overhead the Mallards could see flock after flock of Feathered Friends hurrying southward, honking and quacking in the crisp morning air.

"It is time for us to start for the Sunny Southland," said Mr. Mallard, and he flapped his wings a few times to limber them up after sitting on the Duck Pond all night.

Of course the Young Mallards were anxious to see their winter home in the Land of Sunshine even though they loved the Old Homestead. In a moment they were all in the air and flying swiftly away on their long journey. It was to be the longest game of Sail they had ever played.

Mrs. Mallard looked back and quacked loudly. She could barely see the Sheltered Little Cove because it was covered so deep under snow. "Quaack quack-quack-quack" she said, which was her way of saying, "Good-by, Old Homestead."